Students' Experiences of Psychosocial Problems in Higher Education

Around the world, students in higher education suffer from and deal with psychosocial problems. This phenomenon is universal and seems to be increasing. A vast number of students enter higher education with problems like stress, anxiety or depression, or develop them during their student lives, due to, for example, loneliness, family crisis, mental health or study environment issues.

Battling, belonging and recognition are the focal points of this book's analyses, showing how students faced with psychosocial problems experience high degrees of stigma and exclusion in the academic communities and society as such. The book is based on research situated in a welfare society, Denmark, where students have relatively easy access to higher education and to public support for education as well as special support for students with psychosocial problems. Taking a student perspective, the book provides in-depth, qualitative analyses of what characterizes student life, which specific psychosocial and other problems students experience, how problems are constructed, represented and become significant in relation to studying and, not least, how students deal with them.

It will be of great interest to researchers, academics and postgraduate students in the fields of educational psychology, sociology of education and higher education. It will also be of interest to supervisors and administrators in higher education.

Trine Wulf-Andersen is Associate Professor of youth, education and participatory research at Roskilde University, Denmark.

Lene Larsen is Associate Professor of youth, education and welfare at Roskilde University, Denmark.

Annie Aarup Jensen is Associate Professor of learning theory and didactics at Aalborg University, Denmark.

Lone Krogh is Associate Professor of Higher Education policies and practices, teaching and learning at Aalborg University, Denmark.

Aske Basselbjerg Stigemo is a postdoc researcher of education and learning, identity and time-environments at Roskilde University, Denmark.

Mathias Hulgård Kristiansen is PhD fellow of education, mental health and participatory research at Roskilde University, Denmark.

Routledge Research in Higher Education

Student Carers in Higher Education
Navigating, resisting and reinventing academic cultures
Edited by Genine Hook, Marie-Pierre Moreau and Rachel Brooks

A Philosophical Approach to Perceptions of Academic Writing Practices in Higher Education
Through a glass darkly
Amanda French

Title IX and the Protection of Pregnant and Parenting College Students
Identifying Effective Communication and Support Practices
Catherine L. Riley, Alexis Hutchinson, and Carley Dix

Higher Education, State Repression, and Neoliberal Reform in Nicaragua
Reflections from a University under Fire
Edited by Wendi Bellanger, Serena Cosgrove, and Irina Carlota Silber

The Past, Present, and Future of Higher Education in the Arabian Gulf Region
Critical Comparative Perspectives in a Neoliberal Era
Edited by Awad Ibrahim and Osman Z. Barnawi

Students' Experiences of Psychosocial Problems in Higher Education
Battling and Belonging
Edited by Trine Wulf-Andersen, Lene Larsen, Annie Aarup Jensen, Lone Krogh, Aske Basselbjerg Stigemo, Mathias Hulgård Kristiansen

Dismantling Constructs of Whiteness in Higher Education
Narratives of Resistance from the Academy
Edited by Teresa Y. Neely and Margie Montañez

For more information about this series, please visit: www.routledge.com/Routledge-Research-in-Higher-Education/book-series/RRHE

Students' Experiences of Psychosocial Problems in Higher Education
Battling and Belonging

Edited by Trine Wulf-Andersen,
Lene Larsen, Annie Aarup Jensen,
Lone Krogh, Aske Basselbjerg Stigemo
and Mathias Hulgård Kristiansen

LONDON AND NEW YORK

First published 2023
by Routledge
4 Park Square, Milton Park, Abingdon, Oxon OX14 4RN

and by Routledge
605 Third Avenue, New York, NY 10158

Routledge is an imprint of the Taylor & Francis Group, an informa business

© 2023 selection and editorial matter, Trine Wulf-Andersen, Lene Larsen, Annie Aarup Jensen, Lone Krogh, Aske Basselbjerg Stigemo and Mathias Hulgård Kristiansen; individual chapters, the contributors

The right of Trine Wulf-Andersen, Lene Larsen, Annie Aarup Jensen, Lone Krogh, Aske Basselbjerg Stigemo and Mathias Hulgård Kristiansen to be identified as the author[/s] of the editorial material, and of the authors for their individual chapters, has been asserted in accordance with sections 77 and 78 of the Copyright, Designs and Patents Act 1988.

All rights reserved. No part of this book may be reprinted or reproduced or utilised in any form or by any electronic, mechanical, or other means, now known or hereafter invented, including photocopying and recording, or in any information storage or retrieval system, without permission in writing from the publishers.

Trademark notice: Product or corporate names may be trademarks or registered trademarks, and are used only for identification and explanation without intent to infringe.

British Library Cataloguing-in-Publication Data
A catalogue record for this book is available from the British Library

Library of Congress Cataloging-in-Publication Data
A catalog record for this book has been requested

ISBN: 978-1-032-11683-9 (hbk)
ISBN: 978-1-032-11684-6 (pbk)
ISBN: 978-1-003-22102-9 (ebk)

DOI: 10.4324/9781003221029

Typeset in Galliard
by Apex CoVantage, LLC

Contents

List of contributors vi
Acknowledgements viii

1 Battling and belonging. Students' psychosocial problems and the experience of higher education 1

2 Higher education as a battlefield. Contradictions in the Danish educational context 20

3 The orientation towards a student perspective. Methodological framework 36

4 "If I look at myself . . ." Poetic representations of students' negotiations of self 51

5 "Like everyone else can." Shameful identities and the narrative of the 'good student' in higher education 78

6 "I cannot even set the pace." Asynchronicity and inequality in an accelerated educational system 96

7 "If you don't feel at ease socially." Recognition, loneliness and communities in higher education 110

8 "I see it as an extra job I have." Students' extra work in making higher education accessible 125

9 From battling to belonging in higher education 140

Appendix 156
Index 161

Contributors

Annie Aarup Jensen is Associate Professor of learning theory and didactics. She is senior researcher in the *Student Life Project: Psychosocial problems, identity processes and communities in Danish higher education*. She is part of the research group Center for Education Policy Research and the research programme Research in Higher Education at Aalborg University, Denmark. She has an MA in French and Psychology and a PhD in Intercultural Competence in Theory and Practice. Her primary research fields are learning processes in higher education, student-centred and student-directed learning processes, problem-orientation, co-creation, culture and emotions in education and learning.

Aske Basselbjerg Stigemo is postdoc researcher in the *Student Life Project*. He is a member of the research group LEAP (Learning, Education and Pedagogy) at the Department of People and Technology at Roskilde University, Denmark. He has a Master in Work-Life Studies and Philosophy, and a PhD in Work-life Studies and Lifelong Learning. He works in the fields of feminist theory, critical theory and institutional ethnographies. He has a special interest in qualitative methodologies for research into young people's sense of place and belonging. His primary research fields are educational research, learning processes, negotiations of identity and belonging, time and time-environments, and use of participative methods in research.

Lene Larsen is Associate Professor of youth, education and welfare and senior researcher in the *Student Life Project*. She is part of the research group LEAP (Learning, Education and Pedagogy) at the Department of People and Technology at Roskilde University, Denmark. She has a master's in Danish Literature and Pedagogy, and a PhD in Social inclusion and Lifelong Learning. Her primary research fields are marginalized youth, identity and belonging, mental health, young people's educational choices and transitions, learning processes, culture and societal and political policy and participation.

Lone Krogh is Associate Professor of Higher Education policies and practices, teaching and learning. She is senior researcher in the *Student Life Project:* She is a part of the research groups Processes and Learning in Organizations and the Center for Education Policy Research, She was for nine years Head of Learning Lab at Aalborg University, Denmark, with responsibility for teacher training and development and research in the area. She has an MA degree in Policies and Administration. Her main research field is higher education policies and their impact on organizational development, framing teaching and learning practices, problem-based learning, students as partners and co-creation.

Mathias Hulgård Kristiansen is PhD fellow in the *Student Life Project*. He is part of the research group LEAP (Learning, Education and Pedagogy) at Roskilde University, Denmark. He has a master's degree in Welfare Policies and Management. His primary research fields are welfare policies, education, mental health and (youth) participation in research.

Trine Wulf-Andersen is Associate Professor of youth, welfare and participatory research and the manager of the *Student Life Project*. She is part of the research group LEAP (Learning, Education and Pedagogy) and head of the Master Programme in Social Intervention at Roskilde University, Denmark. She has a master's degree in Social Anthropology and a PhD in Social Inclusion and Lifelong Learning. Her primary research fields are education and learning processes, identity and belonging, mental health, well-being and (youth) participation in research.

Acknowledgements

This book is the product of three years' research in the *Student Life Project: Psychosocial problems, identity processes and communities in Danish higher education*. We would like to thank a number of people for their participation in and active contribution to the research project. First and foremost, we wish to thank all the students who were generous with their experiences, thoughts and time during our fieldwork and found the energy to participate in recurring interviews despite being busy studying or dealing with difficult life situations. Their contribution is the heart and cornerstone of the research project and this book. We would also like to thank the project's partners from student organizations and student counselling units at universities and university colleges in Denmark, who shared their knowledge and experience with us in project workshops and in the *Student Life Project's* advisory group. We are grateful for the inspiring discussions and constructive feedback we have received from colleagues in our respective research groups at Roskilde University and Aalborg University. In particular, we owe great thanks to Søren Salling Weber for his contributions in the early phases of the project and his continued engagement in the project group's discussions. Finally, we would like to extend our gratitude to Routledge for editorial advice on this book, and especially to the Velux Foundations, Roskilde University and Aalborg University for funding our research, thus making important research efforts possible.

1 Battling and belonging. Students' psychosocial problems and the experience of higher education

The purpose of this book is to bring student perspectives on students' psychosocial problems to the foreground. Over the last five to ten years, increasing reports of mental health problems amongst students in higher education have been a cause of alarm in many countries. In our work, not only as researchers but also as teachers, academic and/or special pedagogical supervisors and programme managers in higher education, we can also see how students struggle. We, the six authors, are all researchers in the field of educational studies who share a deep interest in students and their identity and learning processes. The ambition of the research project behind the present book was to explore and analyse how different students experience a range of psychosocial problems.

While we were preparing our research project, a student sent a quote to one of us. This quote has become a recurring motif for us. We allude to it with the book's title, and its assertion is a common theme in the questions asked in the analyses in the various chapters. The quote reads as follows[1]: "Everyone you meet is fighting a battle you know nothing about. Be kind. Always."

The student who sent it wanted to emphasize the positive, significant and unexpected experience she had of finding understanding at the university, at a time when she was struggling with many difficult things in her life. As much as we delighted in this heart-warming story, we were worried and saddened by the implicit criticism: that finding understanding and kindness at the university was unexpected and unprecedented for this student. The quote captures, in our view, the important message also urgently present in our research interviews that higher education often knows too little about its students' battles and does not acknowledge the knowledge, time, strength and courage it takes to fight these battles. The quote extends to an imperative of continuously relating to students with the kindness of the courteous realization that we do not always know, we do not know it all.

We have made it our research ambition to explore how students experiencing psychosocial problems struggle in many different ways and on many levels within and outside higher education. The book builds on qualitative, in-depth research of students' experiences of and perspectives on psychosocial problems in higher education. In a longitudinal design, we have followed 47 Danish students over approximately two years. The students are 35 women and 12 men, most of

DOI: 10.4324/9781003221029-1

them aged 27–29 years, from different study programmes across seven Danish universities and university colleges. Qualitative research knowledge of student experiences, representing student perspectives on problems and needs in nuanced ways, is necessary for the long-term development of higher education practices that are better equipped to prevent and ease (the consequences of) psychosocial problems.

The starting point of our book is that defining and approaching the problem as a question of students' mental health in a narrow clinical sense is inadequate. We must understand students' problems in relation to broader conditions for participation, recognition and belonging in higher education. Accordingly, the book provides analyses dedicated to produce knowledge and better understanding of the battles related to specific psychosocial problems and broad everyday situations that are pointed out by students. It also encourages a curious, inquiring and explorative approach to students' perspectives, as we want to learn more about their student life and experiences. What psychosocial problems do students identify? How do they understand them? How do students find that their psychosocial problems intensify or decrease, are understood or stigmatized, or even that they originate from the encounter with higher education programmes and systems, with its teachers, counsellors and other students? What efforts do students muster to establish and maintain a foothold and set a direction in higher education and their own lives?

Discussing these questions, the book explores students' battles regarding shame, time, community and extra work, dynamics of (mis)recognition and belonging and students' perspectives on what conditions would help reduce and remedy their psychosocial problems and support belonging in higher education.

Representing the problem as *psychosocial*

As mentioned earlier, psychosocial problems related to higher education have gained more attention in recent years. What has been called the 'university mental health crisis'[2] has been in focus, as the numbers of students reporting mental health problems like stress, anxiety and depression have increased considerably. Turning to the magnitude of the problem, young people's mental health problems have generally been increasing in Western countries, and in the Nordic countries mental health has become the most important health concern in young people (Kolouh-Söderlund & Lagerkranz, 2016). Student organizations, student counsellors as well as research report very high numbers of higher education students with mental health problems. A survey conducted by the Danish Ministry of Higher Education and Science showed that one in five Danish students 'always' or 'generally' experienced high levels of stress related to studying (Danish Ministry of Higher Education and Science, 2019). Empirical research data show that university students are a 'very high-risk population' for psychological distress and mental disorders, with up to one-third of all students in higher education suffering from mental health issues (Eisenberg et al., 2013; Lacombe et al., 2016; Orygen, 2017; Royal College of Psychiatrists, 2011; Stallman, 2010). For instance,

Baik et al. (2019) refer to a study of about 6,500 students at selected Australian universities that documents high levels of psychological distress amongst 84% of the students. Further, studies in USA (Eisenberg et al., 2013) and in the UK (Royal College of Psychiatrists, 2011) document a higher prevalence and more significant burden of mental health difficulties amongst tertiary students than in society at large (Baik et al., 2019; Ibrahim et al., 2013). However, it is difficult to gain a clear idea of the extent of the problem. Methods of recording data, conducting surveys and performing research vary considerably in scope, depth, categorizations and systems, reflecting the fact that specific problems dealt with as mental health issues are rather different in nature. This is partly because mental health problems in general are known to be associated with stigma, taboos and numerous unreported cases. Recently, the COVID-19 pandemic with its restrictions and reverberations has disturbed the picture, and it is still unclear what will be the long-term impact on student psychosocial problems, the educational sector and student lives.

According to Thomas (2012), the focus on mental health has drawn attention to a particular group of students in higher education, and one desired result is a positive attitude towards more students with mental health problems and an orientation towards support of general student well-being. However, the debate on the 'university mental health crisis' mainly addresses problems in terms of research, policy and practice, within a field of mental health primarily dominated by a strong biomedical paradigm. As Rose (2019) points out, this encourages a formulation of the problem and a framing of a broad range of student well-being discussions and initiatives in terms of mental health or illness and/or psychiatric diagnoses, rather than in terms of learning and pedagogy, participation and inequalities in education. McLeod and Wright discuss how the less diagnostically charged focus on well-being is often associated with (normative) notions of an ideal state of being and "framed by a sense of alarm and grave concerns about how young people are faring, with an associated and pervasive policy logic that action should be taken" (McLeod & Wright, 2015, p. 2). They emphasize that the concept of well-being, which at first glance appears to be a solid and more sociological construct, on closer inspection seems ambiguous and fragmented, and is put to use in different ways for different purposes (McLeod & Wright, 2015, p. 3), sometimes closely intertwined with more biomedical, diagnostic categories. Explaining students' well-being problems in statistical variables, or in biomedical, neurological, biological or diagnostic models, often leads to narrow understandings and representations of social pathologies, in which the categories become the explanatory factors (Beresford, 2020; Willig & Østergaard, 2005). McLeod and Wright aim to rethink youth well-being with a critical examination of how normative understandings, individualization and pathologization of social problems and structural conditions and neoliberal responsibilization frame and affect young people's experience. They argue for "the need to ground policy and educational approaches in the reality of young people's experiences" (McLeod & Wright, 2015, p. 7). The critical research approach also advocates an orientation towards the open exploration of students' own experiences of what they consider the problem to be and for whom. Importantly, this includes acknowledging that psychosocial problems can be experienced as trauma, crisis, loss and suffering but simultaneously associated with meaning, agency, learning and identity (Harper, 2004; Heney, 2020). Along these lines, we argue that defining the problem as students' mental health issues in itself is inadequate, and that students' problems must be understood in relation to the broader conditions for belonging, participation and recognition in higher education.

Important analyses and discussion of these themes have been initiated related to the 'widening participation agenda' in higher education. Battles for social justice and equality have been a classical topic in educational research and policy. Under the banner of widening participation, different policy and practice initiatives have been implemented directed at broadening the access and participation of a diversity of students in higher education, including students of, for example, different gender, ethnicity and class as well as mature students, part-time students, work-based students and students with disabilities (Allan & Storan, 2005). Discussions of students' psychosocial problems also play out within this framework, focusing on the equal rights to education of people with disabilities. The United Nations Convention on the Rights of Persons with Disabilities from 2006 recognizes that "disability is an evolving concept and that disability results from the interaction between persons with impairments and attitudinal and environmental barriers that hinders their full and effective participation in society on an equal basis with others" (Retsinformation, 2017). In 2015, the outcome of the International Conference on Health Promoting Universities and Colleges was the Okanagan Charter, the purpose of which is to provide and embed health in all aspects of campus culture. The charter calls for action and collaboration locally and globally, and across administration, organization and academic staff to create inclusive learning environments (Okanagan Charter, 2015). Despite such political initiatives, it is still difficult for students with psychosocial problems to be recognized and accepted on equal terms with other students. They are often represented by way of their 'disabilities,' 'functional impairment,' 'mental illness' or 'psychiatric diagnosis.' To receive support, they often have to prove themselves as 'deserving consumers' of (widening participation) interventions or to demonstrate a certain aspiration or resilience when facing adversity. In this sense, widening participation initiatives are sometimes criticized for being directed at what young people could do (to do better), rather than what higher education institutions, teachers or politicians could do (Eiras & Huijser, 2021). Notably, Wilkins and Burke (2013) argue that the language of widening participation draws on competing discourses, namely a democratic-progressive discourse (equality and social justice) and a neoliberal one (students as consumers), which might lead to paradoxical interventions and dilemmas for students.

The exemplary question guiding the widening participation agenda is how a greater variety of students can experience recognition and belonging in higher education. For most students, becoming and being a student is associated with worries, doubts and insecurity, and in general students just wish to learn and to cope with and complete their education (Barnett, 2007). This orientation is, to some extent, present also in research literature on higher education teaching and learning, which focuses on the development of learning environments in higher education and teaching as a wide-reaching endeavour. Students experience and appropriate the learning environments where they are to develop professionally and academically, based on their prior experiences and their encounters with teachers, administrators, leaders and counsellors, who from their respective positions work to support students in this development (Clegg & Rowland, 2010). Sambell et al. (2017) underline the importance of students as partners, peer learning and feedback and engagement, whereas the significance of the encounter between different students and particular learning environments is central in, for instance, Biggs and Tang's alignment model (Biggs & Tang, 2007), Tinto's student integration model (Tinto, 2017) and in research on first-year experience, focusing on students' transitions from high school to higher education. Holmegaard et al. (2014) point out that students are in an ongoing process of meaning-making and continuously work on their identity to gain a sense of belonging when their expectations of their new programme interact with their experience. Many authors focus on the teachers' role in facilitating student belonging. In a systematic review, Allen et al. (2018) conclude (across variations) that "teacher support and positive personal characteristics were the strongest predictors of school belonging" (2018, p. 1). Others have emphasized teachers' listening and understanding attitudes (Ramsden, 2003), passion and caring for students (Hattie, 2003, 2009; Ornelius-White, 2007), and working to act kindly and create pleasant environments to support a wide variety of students (Clegg & Rowland, 2010), as crucial factors for students' integration and belonging. However, in this line of higher education research, the interest in facilitating student well-being in higher education teaching and learning often focuses on the conditions that enable students to enter and stay in higher education, to learn the curriculum as intended and to become an academic as intended. Therefore, research often has the inherently institutional purpose of identifying approaches and methods best used in different academic areas to ensure achievement and academic integration, and translating research insights into how 'good' teaching methods can help to develop constructive and supporting learning communities. These approaches all seem to be relevant and legitimate orientations for educational research and development. However, questions of student belonging are to a lesser degree formulated from a student life perspective, and analyses of student belonging are rarely taken beyond a higher education context with an orientation towards how learning extends to other contexts in complicated, far-reaching and transformative identity processes (such as in the writings of Illeris (2013), building on Rogers (1983)). Furthermore, this strand of literature does not address issues of students' psychosocial problems.

We find an approach that integrates a focus on student experience, psychosocial problems and identity processes, in higher education and also in other life contexts for students, to be of immediate importance in research on educational inequality. Our research project has not focused per se on restating the well-known consensus that higher education works as a socio-economic sorting machine in society, but our starting point is that factors like class, race, ethnicity and gender continue to influence admission rates, even though recent decades have seen more students from diverse groups enrol in Danish higher education. Drop-out rates and rates of transition from bachelor's to master's degrees also continue to demonstrate a notable class gap (Thomsen, 2021).

Categories and vocabularies that point to individuals' constitution and biography as the locus of problems, and suggest individuals' coping strategies as solutions to exclusionary processes, can conceal how class, gender, ethnicity and other structural dynamics play a part. To include these dimensions in our analyses, necessary steps are the exploration of psychosocial problems in their relation to specific everyday contexts and examination of the collective and societal dimensions of coping with and recovering from psychosocial problems. We set out to explore the role the current focus on students' mental health and psychosocial constitution might play as a new sorting mechanism in higher education, intersecting with the classic categories (cf. Wulf-Andersen & Larsen, 2020). In what ways are institutionalized patterns of inequality influenced, when categories informed by psychological and psychiatric knowledge enter the field of education and student counselling? How do students take on or work to resist divergent, sometimes contradictory, categorizations of their problems? How are students affected by social valuation practices and how do they try to orient themselves in relation to them? How do neoliberal orientations towards individualism, performance and employability intertwine with questions of students' mental health and of diverse students' belonging in higher education? We are interested in which battles students with psychosocial problems fight in higher education and how they fight them, and if for instance they experience feelings of unworthiness and shame, which can also be seen as indicators or 'symptoms of inequality' (Loveday, 2016). These are important topics to investigate without reproducing neoliberal trends and discourses of self-responsibility. It is important to consider how the ways we frame research problems also actively highlight or conceal certain aspects or perspectives, thus contributing to the (re)production or disruption of inequality. We argue that we should be open and curious about the different kinds of battles for identity that students with psychosocial problems are undergoing, and how they intersect and interact or counteract with student life and other kinds of student problems.

Thus, our ambition in the present book is to address students' psychosocial problems in a double perspective. We explore students' perspectives on their psychosocial problems with the intention of nuancing and deepening our understanding of *students' experience of problems*: How do students experience the conditions and implications of being students? How are different kinds of ill-being part of their student life? We also explore what particular categories of and actions towards students' psychosocial problems in higher education settings mean to students, thus reflecting on *students' experience of problem representations*[3]: How are students' problems met and dealt with in higher education? What are the implications of this from students' perspectives? An overarching question is how approaching both dimensions of the problem from a student perspective can generate new knowledge and shed light on new nuances of students' psychosocial problems, and lead to new forms of representation and new paths to student well-being. We provide analyses that show, from a student perspective, how psychosocial problems are thought of, and why students seem "obliged to think in certain ways" (Somers in McLeod & Wright, 2015, p. 5). We explore (policy) assumptions behind problems and problem representations and discuss how students' psychosocial problems could be understood and addressed differently (p. 6). We analyse how predominant approaches to psychosocial problems work on an individual level, and what that might mean for students experiencing problems and their efforts to achieve a sense of belonging and recognition in higher education.

The book brings different students' experiences of everyday student life to the foreground, exploring the empirical details of problems as well as possibilities for change. This entails critical analysis of "the harsh and brutal dimensions of human experience, and the structural and historical conditions that produce them" (Ortner, 2016, p. 49) and also of caring dimensions and the ways people work to overcome problems. This kind of inquiry focuses also on "what gives lives a sense of purpose or direction or how people search for the best way to live" (Walker & Kavedžija, in Ortner, 2016, p. 59). We examine students' own stories and explanations of the impact of having psychosocial problems. The relationship between the subjective and the collective level is at the heart of our choice to use the term *psychosocial problems* to represent the central problem dealt with in this book. When we prefer to represent and discuss problems as *psychosocial* rather than in terms of, for example, mental health/illness or well-being, it is because we wish, on the one hand, to acknowledge and maintain that some students do experience dire mental and emotional processes, which can be characterized as problematic and urgent to address, sometimes in the form of psychiatric treatment. On the other hand, we want to acknowledge and emphasize that such problems always have essential social dimensions that tend to be understated in concepts and categorizations associated with the psychiatric field and individual counselling. The term psychosocial problems moves further to address and understand a range of ill-beings, including feeling sad, lost or isolated, grief, anxiety and depression as well as severe clinical mental illness, as a question of people's subjective experience in relation to everyday practices and social relations in particular social, institutional and cultural contexts. This in turn implies that the orientation towards the student perspective should *not* be understood as a focus on individuals but rather as an orientation towards the material, social, cultural and political processes being embedded in particular students' processes and possibilities.

Representing our focus as psychosocial problems identifies student problems as phenomena that are complex; are associated with a wide variety of contexts, causes and forms of expression and are conceived of very differently according to different scientific paradigms. This definition of psychosocial problems implies that they embrace ambiguity and ambivalence. In formulating a sociological and pedagogical approach to psychosocial problems, we wish to transgress the distinction between structural and subjective levels of analysis in our attempt to understand students' everyday definitions and experiences of problems. Following the perspective of student experiences of psychosocial problems provides a crucial prism for critical analysis of belonging in higher education.

Battling for belonging

The analytical focus on students' battling and belonging begins with the decision to explore student experience. Battling and belonging emanate as powerful empirical categories and student orientations in our data. The significance of experiencing 'fitting in' or 'belonging somewhere' is a prominent orientation for the students in our study. In our experience from researching young people's participation in educational settings and local communities, as in other studies, belonging rings familiar and comes close to young people's everyday experiences of what gives coherence and direction to life, and what engages and matters to them (Cuervo & Wyn, 2014; Larsen et al., 2016; Meehan & Howells, 2018). Likewise, many of the students in our research refer directly to the kind of battles they have had to fight during their life as a whole and in their student life: battles against rules, systems and institutions, against themselves and their psychosocial problems and against cultural values and societal norms and discourses. Other researchers have also found that students talk of higher education in terms of a 'struggle' (see, for instance, Leathwood & O'Connell, 2003).

On another level, battling and belonging represent theoretical concepts, crucial in the rethinking of psychosocial problems as structurally, discursively and subjectively embedded and in the deconstruction of existing understandings at work in higher education. This ambition implies an orientation towards a broad and compound theoretical and methodological approach, containing both realist and poststructuralist perspectives. Our theoretical concepts for students' battling and belonging connect inextricably with our theoretical understanding of student experience, which draws on the German tradition of critical theory, especially the writings of Oskar Negt and some of his successors. The main point here is conceptualization of 'the societal subject' where experience is a process developing in a subject-object-dialectic (Negt, 1964; Nielsen, 1997). This approach considers experience as establishing a substantive place of encounter between subjective and societal dynamics. Experience is the process through which we cognitively, emotionally and sensually appropriate reality. Previous life experience as well as current everyday contexts shape the subject's understandings, interpretations and (re)formulations of phenomena and situations. This conceptualization of subjective experience forms the basis for understanding psychosocial problems as real, even if subjectively they have very different meanings. It also inspires an analysis of situated students' life processes, including psychosocial problems, as linked to previous life and educational experiences as well as broader learning processes and social communities related to higher education and societal dynamics. Here, we are inspired by Dorothy Smith (2005), in rooting analyses in students' standpoints, understanding students as knowers of their everyday life but at the same time oriented towards ruling forces in institutions and contemporary capitalistic society. Working from these theoretical grounds, we focus our exploration of psychosocial problems on how they manifest themselves in student experience as simultaneously biographically, institutionally and socioculturally constituted processes that are constantly developing, as we turn to belonging as our primary theoretical concept.

Belonging, as a theoretical concern, focuses on students' efforts to be/become connected to people, places and issues that matter to them (Cuervo & Wyn, 2014), and an analysis of belonging focuses on how students find a sense of belonging to be possible or impossible for them in different (educational) contexts or landscapes. In our analyses of student belonging, we draw on a range of authors, and in this section, we will present the main conceptual grounds of the book.

With the concept of *(be)longing* (2000a, 2000b), Davies emphasizes the correlation and interplay between belonging, being and longing as a significant ambiguity and fundamentally processual characteristic of identity and of being inscribed in a specific landscape. Davies (2000b) understands landscapes as both geographical and cultural terrains. Experiences and narratives of sensing and being inscribed in a specific landscape constitute important dimensions of experiencing identity, and in Davies' conceptualization, body, emotion, language and social practice are not separate elements. Rather, they are different dimensions of experience (Davies, 2000a, p. 37), intertwined with each other and in material, relational and discursive 'realities,' which must be understood in their historical, sociocultural and political contexts.

With an emphasis on spatial-political dimensions, Antonsich (2010) identifies two central analytical dimensions of the concept of belonging. On the one hand, belonging describes a personal and intimate feeling of belonging somewhere (place-belongingness). On the other hand, belonging is a discursive resource in socio-spatial processes of inclusion and exclusion (politics of belonging) (Antonsich, 2010, p. 645). The question of 'where I belong' is thus connected to questions of 'who I am' as well as 'who I would like to be' or become (Antonsich, 2010, p. 646). Belonging thus implies both the active subject's need and work for belonging and the implications of submitting to a discourse of who and how someone can belong in/to a particular place or community. The distinction between *place-belongingness* and the *politics of belonging* highlights how higher education settings are also politicized landscapes, determining opportunities and limitations for different students' participation and belonging. Belonging is in this sense a multidimensional concept, including, for instance, gender, ethnicity and citizenship as well as body, emotion and language as relevant dimensions of status, affiliation and identity (Antonsich, 2010, p. 645), making belonging unevenly distributed: Not all students have the same opportunities to establish belonging, to be recognized as belonging, or alternatively to choose not to belong.

Belonging can also be associated with theories of social learning (Lave & Wenger, 1991; Wenger, 1998) and of learning as becoming (Colley et al., 2003). Such processes can lead to identification as well as dis-identification with a community. One can identify more or less with a community and the need to belong to it and to be accountable to its regime of competences (Wenger, 1998). Participation in communities of practice entails membership and belonging established over time through the development of mutual engagement, shared enterprise and shared repertoire, processes through which students develop and negotiate meaning and identity (Wenger, 1998). These inspirations employ a focus on learning, where the formal content and subject matter of education are not the defining factors in young people's identity formation. Rather, they emphasize participation in everyday practices as the focal point for identity and meaning. In Wenger's (1998) understanding, identities develop through affiliation with local communities of practice, but when, for example, participation in education includes interpretations of structures and purposes outside local educational communities, one at the same time participates in social processes and configurations that extend beyond the local, such as battles for belonging with friends and family and/or as a full member of society. To understand such processes, Wenger points to three different *modes of belonging: engagement, fantasy and alignment.* Related to (higher) educational settings, these modes call for, respectively, local communities for students to engage in, materials and experiences through which they can imagine the world and themselves in it and ways in which they can affect the world and understand their actions as significant (Wenger, 1998). Wenger thus understands learning as participation in social practice, which involves membership and belonging both as practical physical participation and as relations to other individuals.

Similarly, Gravett and Ajjawi (2021) conceptualize *belonging(ness)* as "situated practice" and "a constellation of relations, intimately entangled with identities, becoming and learning" (p. 7). Belonging unfolds in relation to the curriculum and academic content, social relations with teachers, administrators, leaders and other students, the physical places and spaces of the university and campus and the broader institutional culture. Gravett and Ajjawi wish to analyse the social, cultural and physical landscapes (un)available for particular students' belonging, and the implications of different contexts and power relations in/surrounding these landscapes for students' belonging, identity processes and possibilities for action. They also agree that the concept of belonging calls for analysis of intersubjective, institutional and societal levels. However, Gravett and Ajjawi bring to the table a critique of discussions of belonging that subscribe to humanist, individualized understandings of experience for assuming that belonging is something that "can be achieved," which centres attention on "the human as agentic individual" (Gravett & Ajjawi, 2021, p. 5). According to Gravett and Ajjawi, this kind of approach gives inadequate consideration to the impact of space, place, time and wider contexts on student engagement and, furthermore, omits discussion of "the multiplicity of experiences, values and connections that constitute belonging" (p. 5).

There is an immensely important point made here. Establishing a sense of belonging is a complex, reciprocal process, which cannot be isolated to simple questions of 'onboarding' or 'retention' or understood as a straightforward marker of a positive first-year experience, even though these dimensions are relevant aspects of higher education practice and the establishment of student belonging. Gravett and Ajjawi's critical examination of assumptions of belonging as "a universal and uniform experience" is highly appropriate (Gravett & Ajjawi, 2021, p. 3).

With belonging as a multidimensional concept, including students' subjective processes of being, becoming and longing, and the political processes of inclusion and exclusion from places and communities, we are able to embrace and discuss students' identity work and student diversity and analyse "the subtle ways in which students may be marginalised" (Gravett & Ajjawi, 2021, p. 3).

'Good students' and recognition structures of belonging

The focus on belonging directs analytical attention towards the different ideas and concepts of 'the student' in higher education, which are present in discourses, institutions and social dynamics surrounding the students we meet in our research. Domina et al. (2017), for example, show how classifications reproduce the social affiliation of students without them being aware of it, and how this leads to sorting and exclusion processes, indicating who count as legitimate participants, that is, 'good students,' in education. Higher education institutions, campuses, welcoming and retention strategies and ways of teaching and facilitating student communities all imply a particular kind of student (Ulriksen, 2009) or promote tacit assumptions of who belong in higher education and what they are expected to belong to (Thomas, 2015, p. 38). Belonging becomes manifest not only as a subjective, emotional affiliation but also as "a practice and a product of the relations of power embedded in the field of higher education, constructed around the privileged identities of the 'typical' or 'authentic' student" (Thomas, 2015, p. 41). In contemporary higher education, different dominant constructions of students as learners, consumers, (current and future) workers and socialities are at play simultaneously (Brooks & O'Shea, 2021), pushing some students to the centre and others to the periphery as having more or less 'person value' (Skeggs, 2011).

Accompanying the analysis of belonging, thus, is the ambition to explore normative ideas associated with specific educational contexts of who 'proper students' are presumed or supposed to be, what they should be able to or what they must do, because these imagined figures of 'proper students' work to facilitate or constrain students' belonging in higher education.

Along these lines, we need also to examine what happens when students experiencing problems turn to or are referred to help and support systems, professional interventions "designed to re/form those students identified as 'non-standard' into legitimate, normalized subjects" (Burke & Crozier, 2014, p. 54). In what ways do support systems influence students' sense of identity and belonging?

Even though students facing psychosocial problems have formal and legal rights to equal access and participation in education, this could still mean that these students find themselves in a marginal or illegitimate position. Developing an academic identity is formed by logics of employment and narrow understandings of how to be a 'proper' student. Students who are identified as 'non-standard' are often expected to enter processes of self-transformation and self-regulation to become proper students that fit into the dominant educational culture (Burke, 2017, p. 431; Burke & Crozier, 2014). We must include in our analyses the complexity of belonging, including how belonging and un-belonging might coexist for students (Gravett & Ajjawi, 2021, p. 7). If belonging in some higher education settings requires radical homogenization or conformity of student identities, what at first glance seems inclusive and welcoming might in fact contain the opposite, and dissociation or un-belonging could be a positive, active choice of academic or personal integrity (Gravett & Ajjawi, 2021, p. 4).

Approaching students' psychosocial problems through the conceptual lens of belonging, as elaborated earlier, deals with inequality in higher education as formal and informal recognition structures of belonging. Our book employs a theoretical understanding of students' subjective experience of psychosocial problems as a phenomenon linked to battles concerning the uneven distribution of belonging. Theoretically, one could argue, the metaphor of battling alludes to Axel Honneth's (1996) work on the struggle for recognition. Social justice and inequality (re)produce themselves in objective institutional differentiation and also by way of the symbolic violence of being misrecognized (Burke & Crozier, 2014; Fraser, 2001; Honneth, 1996; Skeggs, 1997). Drawing on Nancy Fraser's work (2001, 2008), we can place students' battles for belonging in a greater perspective of inequality and social justice. Fraser argues that misrecognition constitutes status subordination and denies some individuals and groups the opportunity to participate on a par with others in social interaction, social relations and consequently in institutionalized patterns of cultural value (Fraser, 2001). When students struggle to decode and meet expectations related to ideas of 'proper students' and experience (mis)recognition in a variety of forms in educational settings, it affects their sense of belonging and student identity. In our analyses of student belonging, therefore, we focus on the intrapersonal and interpersonal dimensions of recognition and misrecognition, but understand these as inextricably linked to structural powers and discourses. For this reason, we are interested in exploring the relationship between students' local psychosocial or educational problems and more general, existential problems relating to becoming and being a member of society. We must therefore ask how students with psychosocial problems carry and invest academic, social and personal resources in order to actively realize a sense of belonging and find recognition in intimate relations with family and friends (love), in a legal rights and institutional sense (justice) and in becoming a full, worthy member of society (sociality) (Honneth, 1996). On the other hand, we should also devote close attention to how certain student subjects are identified as (un)worthy and, for instance, how this produces intense feelings of shame (Burke, 2017; Frost, 2016; Skeggs, 2011).

Contribution and the chapters of the book

In Denmark, compared with many other countries, the conditions for students in general are quite favourable, regarding, for instance, access to higher education and to public funding of education. Students with mental (or physical) illness or disabilities are entitled to special support to ensure participation on equal terms, to allow them to complete their education in a similar way to other students. It is therefore surprising that a high proportion of Danish students also seem to suffer from psychosocial problems. Belonging as our overarching concept directs attention to students' conditions and opportunities for participation, belonging and recognition in the contexts in and around higher education where their social practices unfold. The main focus on student experience consequently highlights the situated lives of students, institutional frameworks and cultures in higher education, and the societal dynamics and discourses on students and psychosocial problems in a particular historical and political context. This is a context in which identity processes, learning processes and psychosocial problems are produced, unfolded and experienced in particular/different ways (Larsen et al., 2016; Tew, 2011; Wulf-Andersen & Larsen, 2013).

Following our presentation of our leading research questions and theoretical orientation in this opening chapter, the next chapter, *Higher education as a battlefield. Contradictions in the Danish educational context*, presents central features of the context of contemporary Danish higher education. We analyse important changes in European and Danish higher education policies and the most extensive national reforms focusing on progress and competition and discuss how they have affected students' battles for belonging and recognition. We show how discourses on equality and economy have developed and challenged each other with regard to ideals of the welfare state, implementation of new public management and neoliberal policies. The close connection between education and economic planning as part of a modernization programme is linked to international politics and discourses framing the role of the state in a globalized and competitive world. We argue that universities have an ambivalent relation to the question of who belongs in higher education and that this involves navigating contradictory policy discourses.

The third chapter, *The orientation towards a student perspective. Methodological framework*, unfolds how we have investigated psychosocial problems, belonging and recognition from a student perspective. The analyses in this book are based on a longitudinal, ethnographically and biographically informed research project with 47 Danish students. We present the research project, *The Student Life Project*, the methodological principle of 'emergent listening' and the methods of in-depth interviewing and visiting student-selected locations. With inspiration from critical ethnography, we argue for an open, curious approach to students' stories and their orientation and navigation through different contexts of higher education. Finally, we present our analytical approach, which moves from thick descriptions to thematic analysis in an attempt to represent different understandings of how a life with psychosocial problems appears to students battling for belonging in higher education.

In Chapter 4, *"If I look at myself." Poetic representations of students' negotiations of self*, we present a series of poetic representations of students' (re)presentations of themselves. After establishing the problem and purpose of the book, the educational context in Denmark and the methodology of the research project, we break away from the traditional academic writing genre to emphasize subjective and sensory dimensions of the students we have met in our research project. With the poetic representations, research analyses in the visual shape of poems, we try to initiate our analyses in a form that shows rather than explains to the reader how different students think or feel about themselves as students. By giving priority to a more open-ended form of analysis, we hope to illustrate the complexities and emotionality of the student standpoint.

In Chapters 5 to 8, we return to more traditional thematic analysis of student experiences of shame, time, community and extra work when facing psychosocial problems. Here, we continue working with the rich material on student perspectives we have presented.

Chapter 5, *"Like everyone else can." Shameful identities and the narrative of the 'good student' in higher education*, shows how students' experiences of exclusion sometimes turn to individual, inward feelings of unworthiness and shame and a battle against oneself. We show how student biographies, educational cultures and societal contexts interweave in students' negotiations of and inner dialogues on themselves as 'good students,' on their own value and 'proper' student identity. We analyse shame as experiences of contested belonging, as a symptom of misrecognition, in the sense that it points to cultural and institutionalized interpretations and evaluations, constituting some students as non-standard and not proper. We argue that students' experiences of shame show how domains of the social, cultural and emotional are integral dimensions of learning processes involved in becoming good or worthy members of academic and social communities.

Chapter 6, titled *"I cannot even set the pace." Asynchronicity and inequality in an accelerated educational system*, shows the subjective dimensions of how temporal structures in higher education lead to student inequality and continuous battles against time. We analyse how temporal demands seem to be paramount in students' negotiations of legitimacy and belonging in higher education and society, and how this applies in particular ways to students with psychosocial problems. The analysis shows how European Credit Transfer System (ECTS) time and the highlighting of tempo are experienced by 'asynchronous' students, how time works as a vehicle of social differentiation and how time has become an important signifier of belonging in higher education. The chapter concludes that it is the sorting dynamics linked to time and asynchrony, probably as much as students' specific psychosocial problems, that make it difficult for them to belong and be part of student communities.

Chapter 7, *"If you don't feel at ease socially." Recognition, loneliness and communities in higher education*, argues that negotiations about recognition and belonging are also battles for participation in local communities. Developing identity as a student is also about being visible amongst teachers, administrative staff and other students, and the chapter shows what happens when no communities are available and one feels excluded. The chapter shows students' negotiations of the meaning of student communities and the process of recognition or misrecognition involved in the learning trajectories into or out of communities.

"I see it as an extra job I have." Students' extra work of making higher education accessible is the title of Chapter 8, which is about students' battling for help and support. Using institutional ethnography, the chapter focuses on the extra work students with psychosocial problems have to do in order to stay in higher education and get the help and support they are formally entitled to. Students spend a great deal of extra time and energy trying to reconnect, recalibrate and reconstitute their bodily, mental and emotional states and adapt to what counts as higher education standards, norms and 'properness.' This work is often invisible. Further, the chapter shows how students come to understand their difficulties as individual deficits, as a lack of resilience, the solution to which is to adjust personally.

In the closing chapter, Chapter 9, *From battling to belonging in higher education*, we sum up the most important conclusions and perspectives presented in the book. What kind of battles do students with psychosocial problems have to fight within and outside contemporary higher education? How do they manage to stay in education in spite of this? Who and what helps to produce a sense of belonging and recognition and to support the positive development of student identities? Based on the authors' experience with collaborative approaches in higher education, the chapter argues that it is crucial to insist on and further develop continuous dialogues with student perspectives, across different student, researcher, teacher, administrative and other positions. The chapter sums up the book's central points in an analytical model of questions to work from when proceeding in this way, emphasizing that all approaches in this respect must be locally situated and culturally sensitive.

Notes

1. The student knew the quote, ascribed to Brad Meltzer, from the Norwegian youth drama series *Skam*, where the main character of the series' second season has this quote hanging on the wall of her room.
2. For instance in The Guardian (June 26, 2017).
3. Here, we are inspired by Bacchi's (2009) question: 'What is the problem represented to be?'

References

Allan, L., & Storan, J. (2005). *Widening participation: A rough guide for higher education providers.* Action on Access, University of Bradford.

Allen, K., Kern, M. L., Vella-Brodrick, D., Hattie, J., & Waters, L. (2018). What schools need to know about fostering school belonging: A meta-analysis. *Educational Psychology Review, 30*, 1–34. https://doi.org/10.1007/s10648-016-9389-8

Antonsich, M. (2010). Searching for belonging – an analytical framework. *Geography Compass, 4*(6), 644–659.

Bacchi, C. (2009). *Analyzing policy: What's the problem represented to be?* Pearson.

Baik, C., Larcombe, W., & Brooker, A. (2019). How universities can enhance student mental wellbeing: The student perspective. *Higher Education Research and Development, 38*(4), 674–687.

Barnett, R. (2007). *A will to learn: Being a student in an age of uncertainty*. McGraw-Hill/Open University Press.

Beresford, P. (2020). 'Mad', mad studies and advancing inclusive resistance. *Disability & Society*, 35(8), 1337–1342. https://doi.org/10.1080/09687599.2019.1692168

Biggs. J., & Tang, C. (2007). *Teaching for quality learning at University*. Open University Press.

Brooks, R., & O'Shea, S. (2021). *Reimagine the higher education student: Constructing and contesting identities*. Routledge.

Burke, P. J. (2017). Difference in higher education pedagogies: Gender, emotion and shame. *Gender and Education*, 29(4), 430–444.

Burke, P. J., & Crozier, G. (2014). Higher education pedagogies: Gendered formations, mis/recognition and emotion. *Journal of Research in Gender Studies*, 4(2), 52–67.

Clegg, S., & Rowland, S. (2010). Kindness in pedagogical practice and academic life. *British Journal of Sociology of Education*, 31(6), 719–735. https://doi.org/10.1080/01425692.2010.515102

Colley, H., David, J., Diment, K., & Tedder, M. (2003). Learning as becoming in vocational education and training: Class, gender and the role of vocational habitus. *Journal of Vocational Education & Training*, 55(4), 471–498.

Cuervo, H., & Wyn, J. (2014). Reflections on the use of spatial and relational metaphors in youth studies. *Journal of Youth Studies*. https://doi.org/10.1080/13676261.2013.878796

Danish Ministry of Higher Education and Science. (2019). *Stress og trivsel blandt studerende* [*Student stress and well-being*]. Danish Ministry of Higher Education and Science.

Davies, B. (2000a). *A body of writing 1990–1999*. Alta Mira Press.

Davies, B. (2000b). *(In)scribing body/landscape relations*. Alta Mira Press.

Domina, T., Penner, A., & Penner, E. (2017). Categorical inequality: Schools as sorting machines. *Annual Review of Sociology*, 43, 311–330.

Eiras, P., & Huijser, H. (2021). Exploring spaces in-between: Reimagining the Chinese student in a transnational higher education context in China. In R. Brooks & S. O'Shea (Eds.), *Reimagining the higher education student: Constructing and contesting identities* (pp. 205–222). Routledge.

Eisenberg, D., Hunt, J., & Speer, N. (2013). Mental health in American colleges and universities: Variation across student subgroups and across campuses. *The Journal of Nervous and Mental Disease*, 201(1), 60–67. https://doi.org/10.1097/NMD.0b013e31827ab077

Fraser, N. (2001). Recognition without ethics? *Theory, Culture & Society*, 18(2–3), 21–42.

Fraser, N. (2008). Fra omfordeling til anerkendelse? Retfærdighedens dilemmaer i en 'postsocialistisk' tidsalder [From redistribution to recognition? Dilemmas of justice in a 'post-socialist' age]. In M. H. Jacobsen & R. Willig (Eds.), *Anerkendelsespolitik* [*Recognition politics*] (pp. 58–93). Syddansk Universitetsforlag.

Frost, L. (2016). Exploring the concepts of recognition and shame for social work. *Journal of Social Work Practice*, 30(4), 431–446. http:/doi.org/10.1080/02650533.2015.1132689

Gravett, K., & Ajjawi, R. (2021). Belonging as situated practice. *Studies in Higher Education*, 1–11. https://doi-org.ep.fjernadgang.kb.dk/10.1080/03075079.2021.1894118

Harper, D. (2004). Delusions and discourse: Moving beyond the constraints of the modernist paradigm. *Philosophy, Psychiatry and Psychology, 11*(1), 55–64.

Hattie, J. (2003). *Teachers make a difference: What is the research evidence?* Australian Council of Educational Research.

Hattie, J. (2009). *Visible learning: A synthesis of 800 meta-analyses relating to achievement.* Routledge.

Heney, V. (2020). Unending and uncertain: Thinking through a phenomenological consideration of self-harm towards a feminist understanding of embodied agency. *Journal of International Women's Studies, 21*, 7–21.

Holmegaard, H.T., Madsen, L. M., & Ulriksen, L. (2014). A journey of negotiation and belonging: Understanding student's transitions to science and engineering in higher education. *Cultural Studies of Science Education, 9*, 755–786.

Honneth, A. (1996). *The struggle for recognition – the moral grammar of social conflicts.* Polity Press.

Ibrahim, A. K., Kelly, S. J., Adams, C. E., & Glazebrook, C. (2013). A systematic review of studies of depression prevalence in university students. *Journal of Psychiatric Research, 47*(3), 391–400. http://doi.org/10.1016/j.jpsychires.2012.11.015

Illeris, K. (2013). *Transformativ læring og identitet* [*Transformative learning and identity*]. Samfundslitteratur.

Kolouh-Söderlund, L., & Lagerkranz, H. (2016). *Mental health among young people.* Nordic Centre for Welfare and Social Issues.

Lacombe, W., Finch, S., Shore, R., Murray, C. M., Kentish, S., Mulder, R. A., Lee-Stectum, P., Baik, C., Tokathidis, O., & Williams D. A. (2016). Prevalence and socio-demographic correlates of psychological distress among students at an Australian university. *Students in Higher Education, 41*(6).

Larsen, L., Wulf-Andersen, T. Ø., Nielsen, S. B., & Mogensen, K. H. (2016). Udsatte unges uddannelsesdeltagelse: Tilhør og steder som teoretiske perspektiver [The educational participation of vulnerable young people: Belongings and places as theoretical perspectives]. *Sosiologi i dag, 46*(3–4), 110–129.

Lave, J., & Wenger, E. (1991). *Situated learning: Legitimate peripheral participation.* University Press.

Leathwood, C., & O'Connell, P. (2003). 'It's a struggle': The construction of the 'new student' in higher education. *Journal of Education Policy, 18*(6), 597–615.

Loveday, V. (2016). Embodying deficiency through 'affective practice': Shame, relationality, and the lived experience of social class and gender in higher education. *Sociology, 50*(6), 1140–1155.

McLeod, J., & Wright, K. (2015). Inventing youth wellbeing. In K. Wright & J. McLeod (Eds.), *Rethinking youth wellbeing: Critical perspectives* (pp. 1–10). Springer. https://doi.org/10.1007/978-981-287-188-6__1

Meehan, C., & Howells, K. (2018). In the search of the feeling of 'belonging' in higher education: Undergraduate students transition into higher education. *Journal of Further and Higher Education.*

Negt, O. (1964). *Sociologische Phantasie und exemplarisches Lernen.* Europäische Verlagsanstalt.

Nielsen, B. S. (1997). Det eksemplariske princip. In K. Weber, B. S. Nielsen, & H. Salling Olesen (Eds.), *Modet til fremtiden – inspirationen fra Oskar Negt* (pp. 269–317). Roskilde Universitetsforlag.

Okanagan Charter. (2015). *An international charter for health promoting universities and colleges.* Okanagan Charter.

Ornelius-White, J. (2007). Learner-centered teacher-student relationships are effective: A meta-analysis. *Review of Educational Research*, 77(1), 113–143. https://doi.org/10.3102/003465430298563

Ortner, S. B. (2016). Dark anthropology and its others: Theory since the eighties. *HAU: Journal of Ethnographic Theory*, 6(1), 47–73.

Orygen. (2017). *Under the radar: The mental health of Australian university students.* The National Centre of Excellence in Youth Mental Health.

Ramsden, P. (2003). *Learning to teach in higher education.* Routledge.

Retsinformation. (2017). https://www.retsinformation.dk/eli/ltc/2017/20

Rogers, C. (1983). *Freedom to learn in the 80's.* Macmillan Publishing.

Rose, N. (2019). *Our psychiatric future.* Polity Press.

Royal College of Psychiatrists. (2011). *Mental health of students in higher education.* College Report CR 231.

Sambell, S., Brown, S., & Graham, L. (2017). *Professionalism in practice: Key directions in higher education learning, teaching and assessment.* Springer.

Skeggs, B. (1997). *Formation of class and gender: Becoming respectable.* Sage.

Skeggs, B. (2011). Imagining personhood differently: Person value and autonomist working-class value practices. *The Sociological Review*, 59(3), 496–513.

Smith, D. E. (2005). *Institutional ethnography: A sociology for people.* Gender Lens Series. Rowman & Littlefield.

Stallman, H. M. (2010). Psychological distress in university students: A comparison with general population data. *Australian Psychologist*, 45, 249–257. http://doi.org/10.1080/00050067.2010.482109

Tew, J., Ramon, S., Slade, M., Bird, V., Melton, J., & Le Boutillier, C. (2011). Social factors and recovery from mental health difficulties: A review of the evidence. *British Journal of Social Work*, 42, 443–460.

Thomas, K. (2015). Rethinking belonging through Bourdieu, diaspora and the spatial. *Widening Participation and Lifelong Learning*, 17(1), 37–49. http://doi.org/10.5456/WPLL.17.1.37

Thomas, L. (2012). *Building student engagement and belonging in HE at a time of change: Final report from the what works? Student retention and success programme.* HEFCE.

Thomsen, J. P. (2021). The social class gap in bachelor's and master's completion: University dropout in times of educational expansion. *Higher Education*, 83, 1021–1038. https://doi.org/10.1007/s10734-021-00726-3

Tinto, V. (2017). Through the eyes of students. *Journal of College Student Retention: Research, Theory & Practice*, 19(3), 254–269.

Ulriksen, L. (2009). The implied student. *Studies in Higher Education*, 34(5), 517–532.

Wenger, E. (1998). *Communities of practice: Learning, meaning, and identity.* Cambridge University Press.

Wilkins, A., & Burke, P. J. (2013). Widening participation in higher education: The role of professional and social class identities and commitment. *British Journal of Sociology of Education*, 36(3), 1–19.

Willig, R., & Østergaard, M. (Eds.). (2005). *Sociale patologier* [*Social pathologies*]. Hans Reitzels Forlag.

Wulf-Andersen, T., & Larsen, L. (2013). 'Splittet til atomer' – om unges møder med 'systemet' ['Split into atoms': Young people's encounters with the 'system']. In A. Neidel, C. C. Jensen, & M. H. Jørgensen (Eds.), *Inklusion, deltagelse og bedring*

- *Unge med psykosociale vanskeligheder i lokalsamfundet* [*Inclusion, participation and recovery: Young people with psychosocial difficulties in the local community*] (pp. 18–26). Socialstyrelsen.

Wulf-Andersen, T., & Larsen, L. (2020). Students, psychosocial problems and shame in neoliberal higher education. *Journal of Psychosocial Studies, 13*(3), 303–317. https://doi.org/10.1332/147867320X15986395598815

2 Higher education as a battlefield. Contradictions in the Danish educational context

In this chapter, we present contemporary Danish higher education in a welfare state context. We analyse a part of the Danish educational context in a short historical perspective with a focus on selected aspects of the important changes in European and national policies that have influenced Danish higher education to the extent that they have affected students' battles for belonging and recognition. This is because when researching students in Danish higher education with psychosocial problems, it is important to understand how current conditions for studying and working are formed by reforms and political discourses.

In the everyday life of students and staff at higher education institutions, reforms and political changes exist as an interwoven and often contradictory reality producing different signals about the purposes and goals of the educational practices. For instance, higher education as identified by academic immersion and autonomy and only available for a small section of society has undergone dramatic changes. This understanding is due to structural developments in the educational system such as the huge expansion in education in the 1960s and due to a discourse about social mobility and inclusion (Arnesen & Lundahl, 2006; Blossing et al., 2014), followed by a neoliberal managerial discourse and a performance agenda (Connell, 2013).

As we will exemplify in this chapter, the implementation of management reforms that prioritized logics of accountability, excellence, performance, competition and speed (Harvey, 2005; Wiborg, 2013) involved dynamics counterintuitive to notions of equality, inclusion and mobility. It is thus important to highlight the conditions for participation by students and staff in relation to the previous and current regulatory frameworks and battling discourses influencing higher education. It has been the overall policy with reforms and changing discourses that produced contradictory logics based on contrary ideological understandings. To these students and staff, negotiating criteria for participation, meaning and identity in relation to what they desired or strove for seemed often ambivalent and contradictory (Davies, 2000).

As in other countries, the changes in Danish higher education institutions have taken place since the Second World War in connection with the development of a modern welfare state. Higher education played a major role in the changes to society (Juul, 2006; Korsgaard, 1999; Telhaug et al., 2006; Wiborg, 2013). In a

DOI: 10.4324/9781003221029-2

welfare state context, one ambition of the educational policy engineering of higher education has been to break down inequality-creating mechanisms and develop an education system with more inclusiveness and equal opportunities for all, regardless of social background (Arnesen & Lundahl, 2006). The political attention to inequality has mostly focused on increasing social mobility and on breaking the so-called social legacy, in terms of the role of higher education in social reproduction of economic, cultural and social capital (Bourdieu & Passeron, 1990).

In all the Nordic countries, there has been a strong tendency to widen the participation of students from a variety of backgrounds under the slogan of 'a school for all' (Blossing et al., 2014). Together with general structural changes to the labour market in the West (Archer, 2013), this created huge growth in the number of first-time graduates from families with educationally disadvantaged social backgrounds and a huge uptake of female students compared with the numbers 50 years ago (Thomsen, 2021). Approximately 20% of each year group today receives a university degree and 10.5% of the population between 16 and 69 years of age in 2018 had a university education (Rasmussen, 2020). In 1980, around 4,000 students graduated from university, whereas in 2017, that figure was more than 24,000 (Danish Ministry of Higher Education and Science, 2018).

Today, according to the ideals of the welfare state, students have free access in principle to higher education, but they must fulfil certain obligations and requirements related to their chosen programme, admission criteria and other formal rules, and complete their education within limited time. Students also receive state grants during their education, but many supplement their income with paid work and/or state loans at a low interest rate to be repaid after completion. However, when they are delayed and do not fulfil the inbuilt progress criteria, students risk losing state financial support.

The field of higher education in Denmark is a public good and includes universities, university colleges and academies of professional higher education. Universities offer research-based higher education at bachelor's, master's and PhD levels. The university colleges offer higher education up to bachelor's level for professions such as teachers, social workers, nurses and vocational therapists, and finally academies of professional higher education offer, for instance, building construction, design technology, and marketing economics. Today, the higher education system falls under the responsibility of the Ministry of Higher Education and Science, which lays down the overall regulations for all institutions of higher education. These include regulations concerning the admission of students, the structure of studies, programmes offered, awarding of degrees and appointment of teachers and academic staff. Each higher education institution develops and updates its own study programmes, indicating the aims, scope and duration, and form and content, of the courses (European Parliamentary Research Service (2014). At the micro-organizational level, higher education institutions are obliged to develop and design the curricula in alignment with the overall regulations from the ministry. The governance primarily focuses on regulating higher education on market terms, adjusting the educational outcome regarding the number of graduates and profiles of graduates to match occupational requirements.

Discourses on equality and economy

The trajectory of democratizing education and the interest in developing politics targeting equality as part of engineering education has been an integral part of the welfare state ideology since the post-war era. In the Youth Commission from 1945, the question of equal access to education was introduced, where it was stressed that economic background should not be the determinant for whether gifted or bright youth could apply for further education. It was argued that it is of societal value to have people from all strata of society placed in privileged positions in the society (Hansen, 1997). During the financial boom from the 1950s to the 1970s, the lack of a qualified workforce was seen as a barrier to further economic growth. This drew attention towards the tertiary sector as an important key to unlocking new knowledge resources (Mathiesen, 1974). These overall tendencies resulted in an application boom; there was a huge increase from 14,000 students in 1957 to 71,000 in 1972, which broadened young people's participation in tertiary education (Thomsen, 2008).

In the 1980s, a programme for educational planning called U90 was introduced to provide new ideas on how the engineering or political planning of education could be beneficial in a societal perspective. This was the culmination of the social democratic education policy of the 1970s, because politicians had recognized the connection between education and societal development. The U90 programme addressed questions on how education can be part of the good life and the good society, highlighting the importance of conducting an equality-based educational policy to promote social mobility. During the 1980s, there was a shift in political power, and the equality discourse was replaced by new thoughts on modernization of the public sector. The replacement of a right-wing government signalled the start of 11 years of an educational policy framework that argued for the importance of seeing education as an investment and educational achievements as more of a virtue reflecting individual effort and exercise of freedom.

In the 1990, the ideals of the welfare state were especially challenged by the implementation of new public management. This movement towards market mechanisms and controlling public institutions in similar ways to private companies installed a logic of accountability, performance and profitability. The equality discourse was gradually challenged by a neoliberal ideology advocating individual freedom, market dynamics and competition, transforming the welfare state into a hybrid state between a welfare state and a market state (Pedersen, 2011). This line of fiscal policy continued through the subsequent governments and shifting political ideologies. The equality discourse was dismantled/supplemented by the focus on economic governance seen in for example ministerial rapports like 'Quality in the Educational System' (Danish Ministry of Finance, 1998) and 'Quality to be seen' (Danish Ministry of Education, 2000). At that time, the Ministry of Finance increasingly began to participate in formulating central goals and initiatives for the educational sector.

Human capital theory played a crucial role in the understanding of educational governance in Denmark from the 1990s, although with a different understanding of how equality matched ideologies about the individual (Thomsen, 2008). In 2001, there was an accentuation of the requirement to create more equal opportunities, but this time it was announced within a neoliberal market understanding where the final social position in society was solely based on individual skills and abilities. Achieving prestigious types of education and occupation are in this sense a result of one's talents and hard work where everyone can create a better life if they want to. This indicates that access to higher education and the use of it to achieve occupational success is only the result of individual effort, motivation and hard work. It points towards the individual as a free-market actor being solely responsible for outcomes in life, thereby disregarding the influence of structural factors on agency (Archer, 2013).

At that period, in the 2000s, much of the democratic influence in educational institutions was replaced by organizational structures resembling private enterprises with a board and power to set the direction for the leadership. The government took control of the regulation of students' access to study programmes in order to match educational input of students with expected occupational needs for qualifications. In 2006, the law of accreditation reinforced government control installing the requirement that the Danish Accreditation Institution constituted by the state under the Ministry of Education must approve all study programmes.

Educational policy in the field of higher education has been closely connected to the modernization of the welfare state, with the Ministry of Finance playing a crucial role in the last three decades. On the one hand, under the discourse of the knowledge society and the need for a qualified future workforce, young people were encouraged to take further education despite their social background, with a subsequent explosion in the number of higher education students. On the other hand, the educational institutions were undergoing a new paradigmatic form of control with key principles such as management, privatization, outsourcing, implementation of financial initiatives, contract management and a tightening of the conditions for studying.

This turn in policy has especially been fuelled by a risk discourse that influenced the admission requirements[1]. For instance, the 'Committee for Quality and Relevance in Further Education' pointed out the risk of education having too many graduates that disproportionately fulfil labour market demands. The result was a mechanism of dimensioning regulated by the profession that controls the admission requirement, making it a dynamics of distribution based solely on market demand (Rasmussen, 2020).

From national autonomy to transnational governance

As stated earlier, state governance has created a close connection between education and economic planning as part of a modernization programme since the 1990s with new public management at the forefront. Another substantial part of the change originates from the European Commission and the OECD in developing a discourse framing the role of the state in a globalized and competitive world. As in other countries, Danish educational policy in recent decades has been influenced by orientations towards internationalization and globalization. For instance, in the white paper 'Growth, Competitiveness, Employment' from the European Commission, Jaques Delors strongly promoted lifelong learning as the way to secure sustained growth in the European member states (1994, p. 136). Education and training should encourage growth, innovation and competitiveness and promote further training for employment, thus fulfilling the market demand for a continuing investment in human resources. With a large part of the labour force in employment, Delors argued for developing the concept of lifelong learning and training as embedded in future policy to ensure further growth across the member states by exchanging skills and best practices and fostering innovation in education.

Furthermore, the OECD had a substantial role in changing Danish higher education. This mainly took place through soft governance mediated by civil servants to politicians with a set of distinctive norms and practices from the OECD, grounded in neoliberal market-friendly economic policies. This was translated into the Danish educational context with the use of principles and norms grounded in what is desirable and appropriate for a liberal market as a tuning of education towards an agenda of global competition (Henderson, 1993). The OECD laid down the role institutions should assume in developing and handing on those norms that make actors in each community switch to the logic of appropriateness (March & Olsen, 1989). As such, the OECD routines fulfilled a dual purpose. Amongst member-country civil servants, they created a sense of identity with the interpretation that the organization currently promulgates, such as modernity, market-friendliness, liberalism and efficiency (March & Olsen, 1998, p. 961). This is an educational process and, in a broader perspective, a form of socialization into the mental set of an international technocracy and technocratic rationale (Bassett & Maldonado-Maldonado, 2009).

Educational policy has also redefined the role of universities regarding their societal function. As an example, the latest revised version of the Danish University Act from 2003 emphasizes that universities must cooperate with the local community and contribute to the development of international cooperation. For the first time, communication and mediation with society were included as a general purpose, and higher education was expected to play a crucial role in future innovation and economic development (Rasmussen, 2019). University research and educational results expanded into new areas of responsibility as contributors to the promotion of growth, welfare and development in society. Under the Act, the university as a central institution for knowledge creation and the promotion of culture was expected to exchange knowledge and competencies with society and encourage its employees to participate in the public debate (The University Act, 2003). The orientation towards the demands of society, the national economy, the labour market and the educational institution's role in international competition, innovation and growth became strong discourses to adhere to.

For years, the Danish policy system has not had univocal strategies and initiatives for capturing neoliberal tendencies and motivating universities for change.

As mentioned earlier, it was especially in 2001, when a right-wing government took office, that within the first couple of years, educational policy became notably more neoliberal. The prime minister's speech at the opening of parliament in 2003 confronted the traditionally strong progressive democratic approach to Danish education by saying: "It is like learning of academic skills has been de-emphasized in favour of sitting in a circle on the floor and asking: 'What do you think?'" (cited and translated in Ydesen, 2021). A long-standing democratic inclusive tradition was suddenly swept off the field as the opposite of academic skills, not a prerequisite for them.

Although previous governments had tried to streamline the growing public sector through various policy initiatives, developments at the national level mainly took place in the flow of the right-wing government's globalization strategy 'Progress, renewal and development – Strategy for Denmark in the global economy' from 2006 (Danish Government, 2006). The globalization strategy is often regarded as one of the first Danish collective attempts to modify the Danish welfare model to match international requirements from the OECD and the EU. It involved a greater focus on competence development and lifelong learning in the development of society as part of the global economy. In terms of discourses, the 2006 reform is interesting because the links to educational recommendations from the OECD are very explicit (Ydesen, 2021).

The Danish strategy also followed up on the goals of the Treaty of Lisbon and was thus considered necessary for a renewal of the welfare state. In the strategy, human knowledge, wealth of ideas and work efforts were considered important parameters for using the opportunities offered by globalization and technological development. In that process, a well-qualified workforce was considered crucial to ensure competitiveness and welfare.

This national globalization strategy included 350 specific initiatives for comprehensive reforms in education and research as well as changes in the conditions for growth and innovation throughout the Danish society. The strategy also included several goals from primary school level to the highest level of education. It was explicitly mentioned that 50% of all young people in 2015 should complete higher education. The initiatives were agreed on in a collective labour agreement. With this agreement, the focus on the importance of education, including lifelong education, was further emphasized, as was intervention in educational planning by actors such as the Danish Government, the EU and the OECD. Overall, the change in discourses with the accentuation on lifelong learning and political pressure for more young people to complete higher education placed the purpose of education as an essential piece in the jigsaw puzzle of the transformation from a welfare state into the logics of a market state. Completing higher education was not to be understood primarily as a matter of personal interest in a particular subject, but subjects should be chosen in consideration of the occupational logics of supply and demand.

The 2006 globalization strategy represented an attempt to initiate fundamental change processes in Danish education. This made Danish educational conditions merge with international conditions – and Denmark allegedly adopted some of the problems students experience across national borders. The strategy formed part of the harmonization of education in the EU, as described in the Treaty of Lisbon, adopted by the Council of Europe and UNESCO in 1997, which refers to the recognition of qualifications across countries in a globalized world.

Like archaeological layers of a policy framework and discourses about lifelong learning, growth, competition and innovation, these changes to the educational landscape created understandings of higher education as being an actor in a European and international market of skills and competencies and an important piece in the jigsaw to maintain future growth and prosperity. The changes initiated an effort to harmonize education across European countries, making it more attractive for students to transfer and study abroad as actors in a free market for education, while underlining the importance of gathering skills and competencies from different educational systems and countries. The influence from the OECD has had a great impact on the direction of the Danish national reform policy and development towards making an intricate link between education, economic thinking and global competition. This is one example of how neoliberal development trends seem to affect Danish education in terms of changes in values and organization, which slowly seep down to management, staff and students in top-down processes in the changing understanding of the purpose, narratives and orientations to what matters regarding education (Widerberg, 2015). In this process, the Bologna Declaration had an enormous impact.

European flexibility: the Bologna Declaration

The Bologna Declaration was adopted in 1999 by 29 European countries. The goal was to create a common European area of higher education and a coherent and flexible education system from basic education through high school to higher education, based on the idea of creating new opportunities for coherence and transparency across educational programmes and national borders (Pedersen, 2011). The intentions were to create more institutional initiatives to make it easier for students to choose between different European educational institutions during their studies as well as to gain credits from different programmes at different institutions.

At the same time, the wording of the declaration called for innovative thinking in education using concepts such as transparency, coherence and student-centred learning. Even though the initiatives sounded relevant, the problem was that the development process took place in neoliberal settings, where the prevailing market thinking ended up dominating and changing sensible and relevant pedagogical ideas originating from years of comprehensive international research in higher education teaching and development. However, the visions of the Bologna Declaration also helped to break down more traditional fixed structures and understandings of education, thus working towards more flexible systems with a more intensive focus on the concept of learning and promoting students' learning outcomes as a new paradigmatic point of reference (Pedersen, 2011).

This seemed to allow for new ways of practising higher education teaching methodology since the Bologna Declaration paved the way for a model of education that indicated that no fixed planning systems should or could guide the teaching (Pedersen, 2011). On the contrary, the focus should be on the student and initiatives that in different ways support students' learning outcomes. Innovative student-centred learning was introduced with the reform policy and its new recommendations for best practices. This was based on results from numerous transnational development projects, and in some ways 'forced' the professional educational system and its researchers and teachers to think and act in new ways, including individualization of student learning. It was the idea that the implementation of the European Credit Transfer System (ECTS), with a focus on students' academic workload rather than on the hours teachers teach, should initiate innovative forms of learning environments. Unfortunately, practical experience has been that this way of measuring study activities as European Credit Transfer System (ECTS)-based workload seemed to be misinterpreted in some educational institutions with the implication that this gives teachers too many teaching tasks. This was probably due to the difficulties in changing traditional thinking regarding educational tasks and a resistance against EU policies and because changes take considerable time to implement, accompanied by resistance to top-down policies.

It could be argued that the Bologna model was developed on market principles since it implied a view of students as customers in an educational market who become employable by successfully moving effortlessly across systems and national boundaries. This correlates with neoliberal understandings of the individual as a free and self-reliant entrepreneur and students as independent and self-governing individuals with free choices in relation to education and unlimited future possibilities to construct their personal-educational trajectory. At an institutional level and from a practical standpoint, this has been enhanced by the development of a module structure allowing students to combine their main education with modules from other national or international universities. Many students have the capacity for this, but many cannot take advantage of these possibilities for a variety of reasons as stated earlier.

The Bologna objectives are not legally binding until they become part of national legislation. That said, from the beginning, Denmark has faithfully followed the general intentions of EU education policy, which are now well implemented in management and education practices in Danish higher education (Brøgger, 2019, p. 142). This is in light of the national globalization strategy from 2006 and the recommendations for comprehensive changes in 2015 by the quality committee set up by the then government (Danish Ministry of Higher Education and Science, 2015). The Danish loyalty to the overall strategies from the EU permeates announcements and documents from the Ministry of Higher Education and Science containing recommendations and standards for best practices. Examples of this are the Danish qualification frameworks from 2003 and 2008 (Danish Ministry of Higher Education and Science, 2021) matching well the international qualification framework, a new grading scale (from 2008), matching the international grading scale, the module structure and accreditation provisions, largely based on EU standards.

The EU implementation process is often referred to as a 'silent revolution' and represents a new type of policy with standardization taking place across education such as the open method of coordination, which aims to spread best practices and achieve convergence towards EU goals (European Parliamentary Research Service, 2014). The open method of coordination, which involves benchmarking, best-practice strategies and standardizations (Krejsler et al., in Brøgger, 2016) and the production of data, in that sense stands out as a representative of how 'soft' management from transnational organizations and collaboration changes local educational institutions (Brøgger, 2016, p. 79), creating quite different working conditions for students and staff.

Recent reforms: progress and competition

At the local level in Denmark, the interpretation of these frameworks, along with the continuing focus on economic factors, has led to the creation of extensive layers of administration and systems of leaders and administrators tasked to control teachers and students and to ensure that they operate within these frameworks. In this connection, the government introduced a progress reform in 2013, with the aim of reducing spending on education by getting students faster through the education system. One element was the requirement of studying and exams for students to obtain state grants; another was a stricter framework for progression through the study programmes (Danish Government, 2013). Each semester includes modules worth 30 ECTS, corresponding to an expected working week of 37–43 hours. This was a clear message to students using time as an indicator to send them a message that they must work very hard at the university to compete and complete. This focus on completion rate and the length of studies had a clear link to European policies on higher education quality, but it also represents a narrow approach to the implementation of studies, leaving students with few other opportunities than to push their own study strategies towards more instrumental measures (Rasmussen, 2019).

Further, an increased focus on public accountability using evaluations, quality control and new management methods arose from a quality system developed as part of the Bologna Declaration from 2005 and finally adopted by the ministers responsible for higher education in the European higher education area in 2015[2], to ensure monitoring and control of the study programmes. These initiatives involved further growth in managerial and administrative job categories. In this context, the academic staff increasingly became regarded as what is typically called 'managed professionals,' representing a form of management that broke with a hitherto high degree of autonomy and responsibility amongst academic staff (Rhoades, 1998).

Competition has always been an inherent mechanism in the mindset of the (elite) university. There are competitive mechanisms between research environments, both nationally and internationally, between studies about producing the most attractive candidates, getting the best students and highest grades, etc. This is a neoliberal mindset based on market mechanisms, which governs education and consequently diminishes the focus on pedagogy and supporting environments for staff and students. Teachers and students are seen as different role players in producing learning in market-like competitive environments, managed by different bureaucratic layers and only the fittest survive what could be referred to as one of the prime centrifugal forces.

The current political processes are continuations of the privatization/modernization waves from the 1980s and 1990s in the public sectors with political attempts to manage state economy and productivity by implementing reform changes at the organizational level. Regarding universities, 14 key reforms were implemented from 2000 to 2018, which have taken up considerable time and effort at all levels in the universities (Rasmussen, 2019). This was combined with major changes since the mid-1980s, such as a huge increase in the number of students, reduction in government grants, increased competition within and between institutions, increased accountability, and procedures to expand access for under-represented groups (i.e. more social mobility) (Tinklin et al., 2005).

These trends are reflected through cuts and financial incentive models that reward students' fast track into education to completion, tests, standardization of completion times and grade bonus systems. A further element was to get students faster out in jobs as employable and mobile young people and, by contrast, to punish educational institutions for having students who are delayed or change their study programme. The state management and control based on institutions' results as well as the reduction of basic grants to the institutions seem to have put increased pressure on university staff and lead to increased numbers of temporary teachers. The simultaneous influence from the OECD and the EU-initiated economic and political reforms as well as the national globalization strategy from 2006 subsequently followed by education policy initiatives and changes at universities can be seen as reasons for teachers and students being under pressure, with the associated risk of developing psychosocial problems.

Battling and belonging in contradictions

As presented earlier, it is not an understatement to say that universities have had an ambivalent relation to the question of who belongs in Danish higher education. The matter of incorporating perspectives on equality has not been the main focus of attention. Although there have been different political initiatives to adjust the uptake and the overall goal of education, it has never really been seen as a key task to promote equality based on criteria of, for example, social, gendered, economic and cultural background. Instead, higher education has traditionally been understood as the place for creating the highest and most prominent knowledge, setting aside questions about inclusion, equality and problems of social reproduction. Knowledge production and assessment of qualifications have been seen as the core task. With the increased uptake, the discourse about higher education as the bridge to a better and meaningful life has changed. The need for a qualified workforce in a global knowledge economy with education as an actor in a global market is leading to awareness of the explosion in the numbers of students with psychosocial problems, and initial efforts to question taken-for-granted higher education pedagogical cultures have created an immense cross-pressure and conflicting expectations in the landscape of higher education.

To summarize, Danish higher education has undergone several neoliberal reforms that have each contributed to archaeological layers that are counterintuitive to discourses promoting lifelong learning, having more young people completing higher education, and working towards more equality. The increase in the number of people completing a university degree across differentiated socioeconomic factors with more equality regarding gender and ethnicity can be interpreted as a success story. It is considered as an effect of the Nordic welfare models often associated with the highest educational mobility in the world (Narayan et al., 2018). However, as Thomsen states, higher education is still a component of the production of inequality regarding social reproduction, which today to a larger degree constitutes itself as a social differentiation taking place as a distribution of societal status or prestige attached to study programmes (Thomsen, 2021).

Historically, and despite contrary attempts at initiatives of promoting social mobility and equality, higher education has been analysed as the prime institutionalized form of contributor to producing and reproducing categorial inequality (Thomsen, 2021). It has been described as a 'sorting machine' despite often being viewed as based on egalitarian ideals that all people are "educable and deserve an opportunity to learn" (Domina et al., 2017, p. 312). As other writers on educational sociology have stated, the educational system constitutes one of the most influential societal institutions in introducing individuals to social hierarchies, categorial systems and stratifications by allocating them to different social, cultural and economic positions within the society (Bernstein, 2001; Bourdieu, 1997; Domina et al., 2017).

When we analyse the influence of reforms and changing discourses about what defines or constitutes belonging and recognition in higher education, we must see this as taking part within larger, complex processes of political efforts to steer education. As unfolded earlier, there have been opposing forces influencing the dynamics of higher education, including groundbreaking changes in the representation of women and young people from educationally disadvantaged backgrounds. In that sense, social reproduction, sorting and the emergence of psychosocial problems intersect in complex ways as much more than a matter of fulfilling academic requirements or being a question of social class, gender or ethnicity.

When trying to understand the complexity in the rising numbers of students experiencing psychosocial problems, as a dialectic between everyday experiences and structural conditions for studying and working in higher education, it is important to look beyond explanations of it as solely the result of social background. This framework can lead to deterministic predictions that fail to incorporate the sociocultural understanding of the ways the educational system reflects broader battles and contradictory discourses taking place in society that intersect with complexities in students' everyday life. It can also overlook the implications of processes taking place outside the educational institution that intertwine with changes to the educational landscape.

To a greater extent, it is a question of navigating contradictory discourses, local cultural symbolic meaning-making and handling complex negotiations of student identity against the background of changes to the educational landscape. This dialectic interchange between students' situated everyday life experiences and structural conditions for participation, accessibility and possibilities for identity construction are understood as a central part of students' negotiation of their educational participation and self-understanding of belonging and recognition in higher education – as situated reactions to complex and contradictory discourses and structural conditions.

Between ideals of equality and dynamics of exclusion: Firstly, students are presented with an equality and mobility discourse (everyone can and should become something through education), but at the same time, reforms have exacerbated dynamics of exclusion by exerting excessive pressure on students. In this respect, social inequality is linked to the experience of lack of abilities to fulfil neoliberal imperatives about what is right, valuable and desirable.

Between the education of a widening student body and high-quality research for academic careers: Secondly, there is a contradiction between greater competition and policies of inclusion and broader participation. In order to teach still more diverse groups of students, teachers are expected to be methodologically updated, using various innovative teaching methods. However, it is primarily research, not education, that leads to academic jobs and careers. It is research capabilities and the ability to obtain external funding that are rewarded and create careers. This contrasts with the fact that education of students is the largest source of income of universities.

Between students as customers and educational considerations: Thirdly, tendencies in higher education have resulted in a turn towards profitable economic thinking, where educational institutions are expected to think and act like private companies that sell education, understand students as customers and therefore need to market themselves on competitive terms with other educational institutions. New public management thinking has thus had far-reaching consequences for the organization of the individual institution, for the handling of research and educational tasks, for the working conditions of staff and teachers and for the time to carry out the many different tasks.

Between global elitist orientations and local situated needs: Further, the relationship between the global and the local also affects higher education. On the one hand, higher education must compete internationally through ranking systems and reputation, attracting excellent researchers and publication points (in Denmark called the bibliometric research indicator). Globalization has placed pressure on universities to become 'global universities,' or 'class universities' competing for the best students (Crozier & Burke, 2014). On the other hand, higher education is obliged to contribute to the development of local communities through innovative solutions (a 'double impact').

Between ideals of immersion and new market logics of employability: Finally, it is important to be aware that a kind of conflict arises between teachers' desire for good, effective teaching and demands from the top regarding managerial quality criteria, management and control. The managerial quality criteria tend to be based on management rationales, but clash with the understanding of quality of teaching staff. This process can be explained by influence from the OECD (Henderson, 1993).

Within this contradictory reality, students and staff must try to navigate and decode what the proper student is supposed to consist of (Crozier & Burke, 2014). Students encounter a dominant focus on efficiency and performance within the discourse of employability with the pursuit of the good job and the good life. It is easy to understand that they may experience a form of global competition for jobs, alongside a powerful discourse about the unemployment rate amongst graduates, which calls for the best possible curriculum vitae to appear attractive to future employers. Therefore, it becomes important for students to choose the right education, to perform well and to achieve the highest grades to get the best job and ensure the highest probability of achieving the societal criteria for what counts as a good life. These expectations are strongly supported by Danish educational legislation, which in the wording of the University Act states that its purpose is to educate to the highest international level.

Furthermore, students are expected to understand their educational situation as lifelong learning, as the complexity and unpredictability of academic working life entail a need for flexibility, adaptability and the ability to 'learn' and acquire new knowledge and skills. Generally, students are being educated for non-existing positions and job functions (Bowden & Marton, 2003), which of course involves elements of both insecurity and the need to believe in oneself and the future. For many, this can be a demanding and emotionally complex situation. Studies with a clear orientation towards a particular profession such as doctor, engineer, teacher or nurse may involve less uncertainty regarding the labour market, but the lifelong learning expectations will be the same.

From these perspectives, it is not difficult to understand some students' experiences of uncertainty, doubt and stress. Insecurity and anxiety may arise from the awareness of living in a country with favourable possibilities for education financially, but where one is increasingly asked whether one is good enough, fast enough, employable enough, with enough experience from the study programme and from student jobs, and whether one manages to stand out, with high enough marks.

Notes

1 In principle, all young people who have completed high school (gymnasium) have formal access to a higher education programme. Admission is determined by the applicant's high school grade point average as the primary institutional selection mechanism. This admission system to higher education provides competition between the programmes with the highest admission grades and leads to the framing of some programmes as elite programmes with higher societal prestige

due to the difficulty of being accepted. Many students do not get access to their number one priority, and they are allocated to other programmes and/or other institutional and geographical locations. Therefore, the formally free access to higher education is at the same time a sorting process based on grades indicating abilities and, thus, not a 'free' choice.

2 The Standards and Guidelines for Quality Assurance in the European Higher Education Area 2015 were finally adopted by the ministers responsible for higher education in the European higher education area in May 2015. Standards and Guidelines for Quality Assurance in the European Higher Education Area (ESG).

References

Archer, M. (2013). *Social origins of educational systems*. Routledge.
Arnesen, A. L., & Lundahl, L. (2006). Still social and democratic? Inclusive education policies in the Nordic welfare states. *Scandinavian Journal of Educational Research*, 50(3), 285–300.
Bassett, R. M., & Maldonado-Maldonado, A. (Eds.). (2009). *International organizations and higher education policy: Thinking globally, acting locally?* Routledge.
Bernstein, B. (2001). Pædagogiske koder og deres praksismodaliteter [Pedagogical codes and their modalities of practice]. In L. Chouliaraki & M. Bayer (Eds.), *Basil Bernstein, pædagogik, diskurs og magt* [*Basil Bernstein, pedagogy, discourse and power*] (pp. 69–93). Akademisk Forlag.
Blossing, U., Imsen, G., & Moos, L. (2014). *The Nordic education model: 'A school for all' encounters neo-liberal policy*. Springer.
The Bologna Declaration. (1999). https://ec.europa.eu/education/policies/ highereducation/bologna-process-and-european-higher-education-area_en
Bourdieu, P. (1997). *Af praktiske grunde: Omkring teorien om menneskelig handlen* [*Practical reason: On the theory of action*]. Hans Reitzels Forlag.
Bourdieu, P., & Passeron, J. (1990). *Reproduction in education, society and culture*. Sage Publications Ltd.
Bowden, J., & Marton, F. (2003). *The university of learning: Beyond quality and competence*. Routledge.
Brøgger, K. (2016). The rule of mimetic desire in higher education: Governing through naming, shaming and faming. *British Journal of Sociology of Education*, 37(1), 72–91.
Brøgger, K. (2019). *Governing through standards: The faceless masters of higher education. The Bologna process, the EU and the open method of coordination*. Springer.
Connell, R. (2013). The neoliberal cascade and education: An essay on the market agenda and its consequence. *Critical Studies in Education*, 54(2), 99–112.
Crozier, G., & Burke, P. J. (2014). Higher education pedagogies: Gendered formations, mis/recognition and emotion. *Journal of Research in Gender Studies*, 4.
Danish Government. (2006). *Progress, renewal and development – Strategy for Denmark in the global economy*. https://www.ftf.dk/fileadmin/multimedia/fagligt_ arbejde_fremtidens_velfaerdssamfund/pixi.pdf
Danish Government. (2013). https://www.retsinformation.dk/eli/ft/201213 L00226
Danish Ministry of Education. (2000). *Kvalitet der kan ses* [*Quality to be seen*]. Danish Ministry of Education.
Danish Ministry of Finance. (1998). *Kvalitet i uddannelsessystemet* [*Quality in the educational system*]. Danish Ministry of Finance.

Danish Ministry of Higher Education and Science. (2008). *Den danske kvalifikationsramme for de videregående uddannelser* [*The Danish qualifications framework for higher education*]. https://ufm.dk/uddannelse/anerkendelse-og-dokumentation/dokumentation/kvalifikationsrammer/andre/dk-videregaaende

Danish Ministry of Higher Education and Science. (2015). https://ufm.dk/aktuelt/pressemeddelelser/2015/kvalitetsudvalget-behov-for-gennemgribende-aendringer-af-videregaende-uddannelser

Danish Ministry of Higher Education and Science. (2018). *The Søndergaard committee, 2013–2015* [*The quality committee*]. https://ufm.dk/aktuelt/pressemeddelelser/2013/kvaliteten-af-de-videregaende-uddannelser-skal-loftes

Danish Ministry of Higher Education and Science. (2021). *The qualifications frameworks for higher education*. https://ufm.dk/en/education/recognition-and-transparency/transparency-tools/qualifications-frameworks/other-qualifications-frameworks/danish-qf-for-higher-education

Domina, T., Penner, A., & Penner, E. (2017). Categorical inequality: Schools as sorting machines. *Annual Review of Sociology*.

European Commission, Secretariat-General. (1994). *Growth, competitiveness, employment: The challenges and ways forward into the 21st century: White paper*. Publications Office. https://op.europa.eu/en/publication-detail/-/publication/0d563bc1-f17e-48ab-bb2a-9dd9a31d5004

European Parliamentary Research Service. (2014). *The open method of coordination – at a glance*. Retrieved December 1, 2021, from https://www.europarl.europa.eu/EPRS/EPRS-AaG-542142-Open-Method-of-Coordination-FINAL.pdf

Hansen, E. J. (1997). *Perspektiver og begrænsninger i studiet af den sociale rekruttering til uddannelserne* [*Perspectives and constraints in the study of social recruitment to educational programmes*]. Danish National Institute of Social Research.

Harvey, D. (2005). *A brief history of neoliberalism*. Oxford University Press.

Henderson, D. (1993). International economic cooperation revisited. *Government and Opposition, 28*(1), 11–35.

Juul, I. (2006). Den danske velfærdsstat og uddannelsespolitikken [The Danish welfare state and education policy]. In S. Wiborg et al. (Eds.), *Uddannelseshistorie 2006* [*History of education 2006*]. Selskabet for Skole- og Uddannelseshistorie.

Korsgaard, O. (1999). *Kundskabskapløbet. Uddannelse i videnssamfundet* [*The knowledge race: Education in the knowledge society*]. Gyldendal.

March, J., & Olsen, J. (1989). *Rediscovering institutions: The organizational basis of politics*. The Free Press.

March, J., & Olsen, J. (1998). The institutional dynamics of international political orders. *International Organization, 52*(4), 943–969.

Mathiesen, A. (1974). Noget om de statslige uddannelsesundersøgelsers historie i Danmark siden 1945 [Some information about the history of government educational surveys since 1945]. *Nordisk Forum*, 1–2.

Narayan, A., Van der Weide, R., Cojocaru, A., Lakner, C., Redaelli, S., Gerszon Mahler, D., Ramasubbaiah, R. G. N., & Thewissen, S. (2018). *Fair progress?: Economic mobility across generations around the world*. World Bank Group.

Pedersen, O. K. (2011). *Konkurrencestaten* [*The competition state*]. Hans Reitzels Forlag.

Rasmussen, P. (2019). Higher education system reform in Denmark in the Bologna era. In B. Broucker, K. De Wit, J. C. Verhoeven, & L. Leisyte (Eds.), *Higher education system reform* (pp. 79–96). Brill/Sense.

Rasmussen, P. (2020). Universiteterne på vej – hvorhen? [Universities on the move – but where?]. *Dansk Pædagogisk Tidsskrift*, *1*.
Rhoades, G. (1998). *Managed professionals: Unionized faculty and restructuring academic labor*. SUNY Series. Frontiers in Education.
Rhoades, G., & Sporn, B. (2002). New models of management and shifting modes and costs of production: Europe and the United States. *Tertiary Education and Management*, *8*, 3.
Telhaug, A. O., et al. (2006). The Nordic model in education: Education as part of the political system in the last 50 years. *Scandinavian Journal of Educational Research*, *50*(3).
Thomsen, J. P. (2008). Social differentiering og kulturel praksis på danske universitetsuddannelser. Ph.d.-afhandling, Forskerskolen i Livslang Læring, Institut for Psykologi og Uddannelsesforskning, Roskilde Universitetscenter.
Thomsen, J. P. (2021). The social class gap in bachelor's and master's completion: University drop out in times of educational expansion. *Higher Education*. https://doi.org/10.1007/s10734-021-00726-3
Tinklin T., Riddell, S., & Wilson, A. (2005). Support for students with mental health difficulties in higher education: The students' perspective. *British Journal of Guidance & Counselling*, *33*(4).
The University Act. (2003). https://danskelove.dk/universitetsloven
Wiborg, S. (2013). Neo-liberalism and universal state education: The cases of Denmark, Norway and Sweden 1980–2011. *Comparative Education*, *49*(4).
Widerberg, K. (2015). Akademia. Om styring i den akademiske hverdag [Academia: Governance in academic life]. In K. Widerberg (Ed.), *I hjertet av velferdsstaten. En invitasjon til institusjonell etnografi* [*In the heart of the welfare state: An invitation to institutional ethnography*] (pp. 143–163). Cappelen Damm Akademisk.
Ydesen, C. (2021). Globalization and localization in the shaping of the Danish public education system – discursive struggles in four historical educational reforms. In W. Zhao & D. Tröhler (Eds.), *Globalization and localization: A Euro-Asia dialogue on 21st-century competency-based curriculum reforms* (pp. 85–109). Springer International Publishing.

3 The orientation towards a student perspective. Methodological framework

In this chapter, we present the processual aspects of the research into exploring students' psychosocial problems in higher education. We present our methodological thoughts and their development during the longitudinal research process, and we illustrate the orchestration of methods and considerations regarding representation of students' voices. We discuss our steps from thick descriptions about students' everyday life issues to the analytical process informed by different theoretical strands. We touch upon the dimensions of power and how to listen for the emergent as something different from the self-explanatory informed by institutionalized prejudices and hegemonic discourses. We discuss how we handled doing research in and around the field which we have all once entered as students and later worked in as researchers, teachers and supervisors in higher education.

The alarming rise in cases of students with psychosocial problems nationally and internationally alike is an unknown quantity, which has only worsened amidst the COVID-19 pandemic. As stated in the beginning, the purpose of this book is to bring the student perspective to the foreground and analyse how different students experience psychosocial problems encountered in higher education, within the conceptual context of participation (Wenger, 1998), belonging (Antonsich, 2010; Davies, 2000), properness (Burke & Crozier, 2014) and (mis)recognition (Fraser, 2001, 2008; Honneth, 1996).

Having the student perspective at the core of our research implied working methodologically with a longitudinal and ethnographically informed research design based on exploring how to give voice in the contested field of higher education discourses and norms (Wulf-Andersen & Neidel, 2012). In that sense, we explored how to bring forth under-represented stories about experiencing psychosocial problems in higher education. But as in critical ethnography (Madison, 2005; Thomas, 1993) and traditions of critical and performative pedagogy (Freire, 1970; Willis, 1978), we were aware of the need to address both our own position within the field and how it influenced the maintaining of a double perspective on representing others while concurrently exploring the pathology. Working from a critical standpoint indicates taking a normative stance as the purpose of doing research. It is a form of engagement with the world where the purpose of doing research has a participatory dimension attached to the meaning of creating new knowledge so that it hopefully, but without promises, can help

DOI: 10.4324/9781003221029-3

to change the world for the better. This can be achieved through deconstruction of pathologizing discourses, practices or regimes, through the articulation of a different language to understand reality, through giving voice and mobilizing collective critique as movements of empowerment or through the use of participatory research close to everyday life situations in institutionalized forms of ruling. This will contribute to what Denzin (2018, p. 227), with reference to Paulo Freire, frames as the pedagogy of hope:

> *Hope, as a form of pedagogy, confronts and interrogates cynicism, the belief that change is not possible or is too costly. Hope works from hopelessness to rage to love. Hope articulates a progressive politics that rejects 'conservative, neoliberal postmodernity'. . . . This is a hope that inspires joy, sharing, collaboration, the belief that something new and empowering can be produced together. But hope, while always unfinished, can be smashed, turned into hopelessness, despair.*

When trying to develop a methodological approach to address the experience of psychosocial problems in higher education, it was important for us to maintain a double movement. This involved staying close to the students' everyday experiences and exploring their life in a holistic manner while also understanding psychosocial problems as a symptom of a structural crisis unfolding dialectically within changes to societal conditions of living, acting and dreaming about a future self.

We decided to pursue the dogma of listening to the students' experiences of being primarily students rather than seeking causal or correlative explanations for their difficulties with educational participation as a straightforward result of mental illness, psychiatric diagnoses, childhood traumas or other socially marginalized or vulnerable positions. Instead, we wanted to follow a line of complexity, understanding the multiple factors of students' everyday life as integrated and intersecting phenomena to be understood as developing from and with the student perspective. This orientation towards listening for what resides within the students' perspective as a standpoint did not imply being naive about how experiences of ambivalence and difficulties take place as factors related to social marginalization, stigmas, social class and production of inequality. Here, the influence from biographical experiences, aspects of socializing, prior formative experiences with education, current living conditions and networks and challenges with physical and mental illness are secondary explanatory conditions but still constitute an important part of their everyday life. We also adopt an overall orientation towards how students' everyday experiences take place within structural conditions framed by capitalist and acceleratory dynamics or neoliberal market discourses about employability and lifelong learning (Alheit, 2012; Biesta, 2009). But, this implied starting first and foremost as listeners rather than explainers.

The orientation towards the student perspective is a methodological answer to an ontological question of students' psychosocial problems and an epistemological question of representation of students and their experience of everyday problematic (Smith, 1989). This form of methodological positioning resides within a range of considerations regarding ways of voicing and representing students' experiences using different methods and techniques of explicating prejudices. An orientation towards the student perspective should *not* be understood as a focus on students' deficits as individuals but rather as an orientation towards the material, social, cultural and political processes embedding processes and possibilities. In a critical ethnographic vein (e.g. Carspecken, 1996; Howard & Ali, 2016), we work to trouble the givens and hegemonic common-sense understandings about what a student is and broaden these understandings by exploring perspectives on what people's battling for belonging encompasses. Or as Thomas (1993, pp. 2–3) writes: "Critical ethnographers describe, analyze, and open to scrutiny otherwise hidden agendas, power centers, and assumptions that inhibit, repress, and constrain. Critical scholarship requires that commonsense assumptions be questioned."

In the mass media and everyday conversations with academic staff, we noted how students' psychosocial problems and difficulties in finding an educational belonging involved explanations about deficiencies, immaturity, lack of independence, incapability to structure their work or a lack of discipline to overcome the hard work required to obtain academic qualifications. It was these forms of prejudiced representations of who and what a student is or ought to be that made us eager to explore and discuss the hegemonic discourse about right and proper student identities (see Chapters 1 and 5). The methodological approach was to insist on an open exploration of experiences from a standpoint that did not explain the students from either an educational institutional or psychological individualized gaze as problems to be solved or normalized. Instead, as a methodological procedure, we wanted to work with the students as sufficient knowers of their everyday life but informed by sociological understandings of ruling forces in a contemporary capitalistic and neoliberal society (Smith, 2005). Titchkosky calls this orientation the *politics of wonder* as a mode of resisting the dominant 'why?' She writes: "Moving from 'why?' to 'how?' invites a politics open to wonder – a wondering about that which organizes bodies and social spaces and their worlds of meaning" (2011, p. 15).

Emergent listening upwards as a methodological principle

This form of critique of positivist and authoritarian research practices has especially been taking place within youth research (e.g. Åkerström & Brunnberg, 2013; Morrow, 2008; Wulf-Andersen et al., 2021). The overall goal has been to underline the importance of taking young people's experiences seriously, pointing towards the awareness of asymmetric relations between youth as immature and incomplete knowers and adults as mature and complete knowers. Regarding methodological considerations, the questions have pivoted around the uneven distribution of power between researcher and informant. This criticism is founded on the troubling of researchers' privileged access to editorial rights, interpretation, and analysis of other people´s everyday thoughts and behaviour.

In continuation of the above, the way we talked with the students had to allow for different narratives to elicit a broader view of who they are, their life trajectories and how their everyday life is assembled. It was the idea that listening for different kinds of experiences as a methodological framework could foster a different representation of students, that is, as much more and beyond vulnerable individuals characterized by deficits and victimized by their incapability of withstanding today's pressure in education and society. This approach resonated with Bronwyn Davies' description of *emergent listening*. She explains: "Emergent listening opens up the possibility of new ways of knowing and new ways of being, both for those who listen and those who are listened to" (Davies, 2014, pp. 22–23). Davies writes about ways of listening as something very much attached to our already established preconceptions of what we think we know or how something ought to be. Interestingly, she describes the classical sociological way of listening as aligned with lines of descent. Descending or downward listening is illustrative of the way in which the researcher as an expert is listening 'down' – not trying to explore the informant's standpoint or perspectives as representing his or her experience of social reality. This resembles Dorothy Smith's allegory of sociology as looking down on people as data from the 14th floor and her advocacy for a sociology that explores the institutionalized power of ideology at ground level (Smith, 2008), rather than understanding data gathering as a matter of finding statements that fit within already established preunderstandings. As Davies writes in the context of research with children: "What we usually think of as listening, particularly as adults listening to children, is most closely aligned with lines of descent; we listen in order to fit what we hear into what we already know" (Davies, 2014, p. 21). In our context of research, adults are replaced with educational institutional logics in the description of issues of student dropouts, retention, lack of study discipline and academic capabilities. The understanding of problems or issues is formulated from the perspective and needs of the educational institution.

Our effort to explore the student standpoint and practise the methodological practice of listening along the lines of ascent was anchored in a principle of being open and curious. As a methodological principle, it was thought of as being the way of practising our willingness to learn about contemporary conditions for studying. Listening and learning from the students' efforts to make sense of educational and societal practices was understood as a result of complex interconnectedness between their broader life experiences when encountering today's educational system. It was based on the idea that exploring their perspectives and orientations as they navigate through the landscape of education could give important insights into the ways that psychosocial problems emerge. Not solely due to developments in higher education or societal changes but as the result of complex interconnections and exchanges between subjectivity and the institutional order or structural conditions, materialized study conditions and discourses influencing contemporary higher education. We felt that exploring the student perspective could enrich our understandings of how intricate connections between life and education would shed light on how they are battling for belonging (Storrie et al., 2010).

Developing a (longitudinal) methodological framework

In a longitudinal design, we followed 47 students from different universities and university colleges over approximately 2 years. The population consisted of 35 female students and 12 male students, most of them aged 27–29 years. In the search for informants, we selectively used framings such as 'Is it difficult for you to be happy?'; 'Are you not happy as a student?' or 'Do you feel like you're on the sidelines as a student?' We used specific words like stressed, pressured or the sidelines to avoid any psychiatric category as a criterion. We made it clear that we wanted students' stories and experiences of being a higher education student. As a result, the students that reached out were battling a wide range of difficulties that had manifested themselves as ill-being or more severe cases of psychosocial problems that entangled with their biography in many ways. In an introductory interview, the students were told that we wanted to follow them over time. The choice of a longitudinal design was based on the argument that experiencing psychosocial difficulties should not be understood as a static condition. This enables insights into students' identity processes and the convoluted trajectories and changing contexts they move through. Furthermore, our thoughts were in line with Beresford's words about the implications of how causes and connotations of mental illness are often wrongly interpreted as individual deficits without paying notice to the complexity of biographical experience evolved through early childhood and youth, the encounter with institutional logics in previous education and structural societal conditions:

> *'Mental illness' constitutes a medicalised individualised interpretation of the phenomenon it seeks to explain, describe and deal with. It is based on a deficit model, which presumes the pathology and inadequacy of 'the mentally ill' and which conceptualises their thoughts, emotions, perceptions and behaviours as wrong and defective. It continues to encourage a search for bio-chemical and genetic explanations (so far with little evidence or success) and the increasing medicalization of many problems, from the problems of childhood to the effects of war.*
>
> (Beresford, 2002, p. 582)

Therefore, in our discussions about our methodological approach, we were keen to understand the students as first and foremost students in their rights and as resourceful individuals. Early on, it was clear that this would not be an easy process. Our effort to develop a different type of relationship between the students and us as researchers touched upon issues of power and authority in many complex ways (Lather, 2001). Being teachers and supervisors, and involved in study management ourselves, we knew that as active participants in higher education.

We were part of the problem and to some extent perhaps biased by our experiences, our theoretical interests and our academic foundation. We were also deeply entangled with the field as self-proclaimed ambassadors for developing a more inclusive study environment, working towards fostering collective learning processes, battling a performance-based study environment, which naturally also involved a normative stance and bias. Processes of mutually challenging our preconceptions, understandings and blind spots were consequently embedded in our research practice in all phases of the project. Our discussions around these reflections raised our awareness of the extent to which, for instance, the powerful discourses of the proper student (Burke & Crozier, 2014) could persist as challenging blindness in our preunderstandings. We agreed upon the need to develop a methodological framework for approaching and being already involved with the research problem from a positioned normative stance (Wulf-Andersen & Neidel, 2012). This would be a methodological approach of listening to students' voices, which could help all of us to be aware of and navigate the dominant logics, narratives and mechanisms of deficit, inadequacy and powerful biomedical and behaviouristic models that harness the conceptualizations of the relationship between mental illness and academic achievements in higher education. The methodological approach was explicitly designed to help us to trouble the idealized conceptualization of a proper student, to avoid having, for example, the disease or deficit narratives at the explanatory forefront and to challenge the individualizing stigmas and deficit thinking associated with mental illness and students' experience of dealing with psychosocial problems.

A way to manifest our position methodologically was to work with a longitudinal design that embraced the biographical trajectory and trivialities and ordinary activities of the students' everyday life. In that sense, we talked about the analytical scope of encounters between different sets of experiences, for example, how their life outside education was shaped by both life-historical experiences and recent or contemporary problems that intersect and intertwine with educational spaces in complex ways. This allowed for understandings of psychological problems as not necessarily demarcated by either the educational institution or activities outside education but as conditions for participation to be understood as situated in an everyday, educational and societal time, setting and space. Thus the psychosocial problems were not only fluctuating and temporary but also a more static and permanent part of their lives.

Based on such an understanding of the complexity that resides in psychosocial problems empirically and analytically, we therefore developed a research design that could encapsulate important changes over time. It was based on the idea that we had to ask around and outside the obvious ways to grasp where, why and how the psychosocial problems evolved. This would enable us to understand students' psychosocial problems as not only relatable to or stemming from the educational institutions but as integrated with their everyday experiences, without losing sight of the effects and dynamics in higher education that activated, enforced or worsened students' experiences of being in trouble, misplaced, excluded or unable to live up to contemporary norms of recognition and belonging. In that vein, we also looked out for glimpses of being seen as individuals and met with help and understanding, as a mirage of what higher education might also be.

These considerations led us to the following focus points in developing questions for our interviews and guide for fieldwork consisting of three individual interviews with the students and a visit at a location of their choosing.

The orientation towards their everyday life: How are the students experiencing their student life as part of their everyday life, what are their routines, their regular appointments and their primary social network; what do they do in a typical week; what kinds of activities do they participate in; what kind of thoughts are dominant and at what times and places? What kinds of difficulties do they experience in their everyday life as students? What kinds of situations and contexts are the difficulties related to? How do they understand and negotiate their life-historical experiences, their 'socialization' within and in connection to the educational setting?

The orientation towards their horizontal and vertical life situation: What are the contours of their historical background; where did they grow up; what are their previous experiences with the educational system; what kinds of memories do they have of life-transforming situations; how was their social network when growing up and what were their obligations, roles and support in their family? What kind of future were and are they hoping for and what role does education play in their orientations towards the future?

The orientation towards their study environment: How do they describe the state of their study programme and study environment and how do they describe their participation, roles and norms in their contextualized study cultures? What are designated activities to do, places to be, work rituals and ways of being together in their programme? What parts of the educational culture enhance or limit students' possibilities for staying and completing their studies?

The orientation towards a place to visit of their choice: If asked, what place of importance will the student choose to show us? Why that place, what are the imminent and explicit stories evolving during the visit, what experience or situation is highlighted as important? How can the selected place be understood as a constructed image and an in situ medium for exchanging experiences of the process of and battle for belonging as a higher education student? What kinds of talk emerge in the place as a situated context for conversation? What do the students' explanations of the place symbolize concerning their student life and experiences of being a student?

The orientation towards their use of personal strategies and ways of finding support: What kind of individual strategies and solutions do the students develop to try to solve or overcome their difficulties? What are their experiences of finding forms of support, for example, private, public and educational? What does this support mean to them? What was the thought behind it? How is it transforming their self-understanding and student identity? Does their mode of participation change because of the support?

Searching for aspects of belonging and recognition in such a methodological approach has been positioned within a broad understanding of experience as both subjective and societal. This indicates that students' perspectives on cognitive, emotional and sensory processes of belonging reside within the subjective as the societal condition for recognition. Education has an immense role in the production of fabrics for societal status and works as a sorting mechanism for the distribution of cultural and economic capital (Domina et al., 2017). This intertwines with discourses of what encompasses trajectories towards recognized positions in society such as being a productive, profitable and participating member of the labour force. Since the importance of education rests upon processes of recognition at the societal level, this implies understanding education as a space for subjective negotiation. Orientations towards a student perspective help us understand the ways in which contemporary norms of belonging and recognition are part of a subjective identity negotiation between the student and society. This starts where the student's standpoint is at a given place and time in their life. It enhances our insight into the evolution of identity processes as complex, changing and contextual as well as relatable to society on a winding course. This is thus part of students' ongoing work towards finding meaning and coherence in their life.

Empirical methods

The interviews

The purpose of doing individual interviews with students was to create in-depth knowledge about their subjective understandings and ways of navigating their student life. These experiences are to be understood as active processes of learning. The interviews were developed within the understanding of what Spradly (1979) amongst others has formulated as a core of the ethnographic interview from the bottom-up perspective: "I want to understand the world from your point of view. I want to know what you know in the way you know it" (Spradly, 1979, p. 34). This implies understanding the world as it unfolds and becomes interpreted from the students' gaze or perspective.

At the same time, we had selected thematic points of interest such as eliciting descriptions of how they used their time during a typical week, what kind of social networks they were surrounded by, how they used support systems or tried to find help and what their prior educational experiences were like. We asked for biographical perspectives as these were found to be meaningful and brought up or indicated by the students when exploring different topics during the interviews, but mainly in the context of changes they had undergone in their life and studies alike. This often happened when we were talking about how they had been affected by sudden illness or death in their family, or they brought up episodes in their childhood or adulthood that had affected them.

The first interview – a typical week

In the first interview, we were primarily interested in how they understood themselves, and we wished to reconstruct an overview of their everyday life. We explored what they did in a typical week and how they felt at different times of day in a typical week. We asked how they felt about their programme, what kind of support they received, what social networks they were part of or had been excluded from. Initially, we emphasized their present experience of being a student.

One of the ways we tried to materialize combining our effort to talk with the students outside the dominant narratives and practising Davies's conceptualization of emergent listening was to destabilize the possible expectations of what we wanted to talk about. We did this by starting with an exercise of marking up parts of their everyday life. We made a simple weekly timetable with blank boxes to fill out and asked what their typical week would look like.

This simple tool was interesting in many ways regarding the kind of stories that evolved with the help of such a simple though restrictive framework. It forced us and the students to start with very trivial activities of how they typically arranged their week, paving the way for talking about normal and abnormal weeks relative to their mental and physical state. It was helpful in forming a mutual ground that suspended dominant assessments and prejudices as the contours of their life in its materiality emerged and unfolded (Rinaldi, 2006, p. 65). We were slowly getting to know who the students were and their backgrounds without too many disturbances from second-order reflective and normative judgemental rulings of what a proper student should be like and to what extent the students found that they fulfilled those criteria.

It was remarkable to notice how their weeks were composite in varying ways and to what extent they could describe and remember what they did on a weekly basis. A trivial finding was how much of their life was influenced by their psychosocial well-being as a student. Another interesting finding was the way in which the psychosocial problems produced in their studies were interwoven with their efforts to practise self-treatment. In addition came the amount of extra work (see Chapter 8) many of the students had to conduct in the form of keeping their appointments with doctors, psychologists and psychiatrists as strategies for getting better or getting the appropriate documentation for waivers or extra support. This included filling out forms for financial support or supported education and the time and energy spent on writing applications for waivers, while adhering to bureaucratic measures that had been tightening over the last decade of structural reforms in higher education (cf. Chapter 2).

Finally, it was informative to learn how they felt and acted outside the actual time spent in their educational setting, what kinds of hobbies they had (so many knitted or went on long walks as a way of controlling their thoughts and feeling calm), what kinds of communities they took part in and what kinds of work they did in parallel with their studies and what the work meant for them as a secondary community of belonging often in sharp contrast to their lack of experience of social cohesiveness on their programme. We also learned how resourceful they were in these other activities in forms of communities that were often much more inclusive, open and oriented towards establishing community cohesion than they experienced at their place of study. Without emphasis on relevant places, activities and communities outside their education, these could have been interpreted as taken for granted and of no importance to the overall understanding of the students' agency. Allowing for a dialogue that was different from expected and that started somewhere else than with education at the forefront made it possible to explore different stories of who they were and what they had managed to achieve or overcome in their life.

Reconstructing a typical week gives the informant the possibility to process her or his experiences in a way that can create a forward-looking perspective (Wengraf, 2001) with a potential for transformative agency, but without making preunderstandings the unequivocal basis for the research. This gives back some of the editorial rights.

The second interview – mapping connections

In the second round of interviews, we focused more deeply on what the students would describe as important preconditions for well-being in their studies. We were interested in what they would highlight as being important positive and negative triggers in their life, and what possibilities and barriers they themselves would describe as affecting their ability to study. We also asked about the first time they went somewhere else asking for help, what led up to the situation and how it unfolded. It was in the second interview that we talked about if there were certain places they avoided going to, with reference to bad experiences. Furthermore, with a longitudinal study, we could revisit our first interview and in retrospect listen for important themes that we found relevant to explore more deeply. Together with the student, we mapped what had been brought up as important relations to other people and communities and important activities that helped describe the student's environment. This could indicate the absence of strong social networks as well as significant others in the form of support from family and friends and important activities and communities that operated as safe havens or even opposites of the study culture. The act of making the map and visualizing on paper the relationships and their priority created a different dialogic situation, where the student's negotiations about where to place a certain person or group of people and why were vocalized, thus giving additional insights into their perception of the complexity of their life. We also touched upon their reasons for their choice of programme, what it meant for them be a student and what they would describe as their motivating force.

The third interview – metaphors as meta-perspectives

In the third round of interviews, besides returning with follow-up questions from the first and second interviews, we made an overview of the student's student life. This was done in collaboration with the student. We moved away from the everyday life episodes to talk about more general patterns, looking at their student life from an outside perspective. Having three consecutive interviews allowed students to reflect upon their student life. We related their experiences of participating in higher education to their life-historical trajectory through the educational system. This led to talk about similarities and differences between now and then and about what could have initiated any changes.

We also asked the students to come up with metaphors, analogies or imagery that came to mind that could describe their process in higher education and to what extent that picture had changed along the way or stayed the same. We also touched upon their thoughts and feelings about them as students, calling for more self-evaluative judgements of whether and how they had tried to fit into the study culture and not stand out as different. Finally, we asked for what kind of advice they wished they had received during the process and how they envisaged their future self.

Visit at a chosen location

Our interest in the students' broader everyday life situation also provided an orientation towards places. We were curious about how site visits, to a place or area selected by the students as being of importance to them in relation to their student life, could focus attention on battles of and for belonging that did not appear equally in linguistic form (Harper, 2012; Rasmussen, 2013, 2017), being for instance more embodied, spatialized and materialized memories of prior experiences. We were interested in exploring places that reflected student life as well as places that could lead to other stories. The students showed us many different places: parks, local urban areas, natural areas, specific parts of educational institutions, a church, their old hometown or where they now lived, cemeteries, etc. In this way, we used visits to places to gain insight into local, situated, material and social aspects of human practice (Szulewicz, 2015). Exploring experiences during visits to places generates a different insight into student life. The location and the visit there constituted an affective relation to their telling of important moments and feelings related to their student life. They were places that mattered, related to situations and feelings that mattered.

But the site visits also had the function of being a methodological approach to enable different forms of representations of a student life and insight into students' subjectivity than being framed by the institutional discourse of properness that inherently was part of the relational positioning between us as researchers/teachers/supervisors who evaluate academic performance and them as students being evaluated. During the site visits, we were able to position ourselves differently from educational representatives and we could initiate an invitation into conducting a more collaborative interpretation of what had formed and influenced their experiences of being a student in contemporary society. It also gave access to places where they were and could be in a different role from that of a student.

Our understanding of places was analytically more in line with what Massey (1994) reminds us of, namely that local places are interconnected with a complex of social relations, local, national or global, that are woven together and call for an understanding of places as physical and materialized. At the same time, they are porous spaces that are interpreted subjectively through involvement in a network of relations to power representations of meaning or ideology in which identity formation takes part as negotiations on the continuum of belonging and longing (Antonsich, 2010). Places in that sense reflect parts of the subjective process of negotiating and interpreting conditions for belonging that explain distinct forms of power and the production of social inequality as also a matter of demarcating who belongs where, so long as the place claims the right to a sense of belonging. There is a distribution of influence and status reflected in the use of space, such as indications of being inside/outside or how the choosing of other places mirrors or reflects the abstract educational and societal process of finding belonging in new and complex ways. Nature may thus be a place of healing or cleansing in opposition to the educational institution as filled with metaphors of being in a battle with oneself, feeling threatened or excluded. Here, we see how places are constructed and used by different groups and enable different forms of analysis about belonging.

Analysing using a student perspective

The above-mentioned methodological approach created thick descriptions (Geertz, 1973) with holistic understandings of the students' everyday life situations that helped to withstand objectification of their knowledge of being students. It was a way of representing the many and diverse parts of their life. It allowed for talking about the obvious and visible part of their struggles as well as the invisible and tabooed, that is, the shameful parts that students in their everyday life often spend a lot of energy hiding due to a feeling of them being illegitimate or a sign of weakness.

Theoretically, the conducting and analysis of our interviews and the site visit were to a large degree framed by the work of Antonsich (2010) and his conceptualization of belonging as on the one hand the "personal, intimate, feeling of being 'at home' in a place (place-belongingness)" and on the other hand "belonging as a discursive resource which constructs, claims, justifies, or resists forms of socio-spatial inclusion /exclusion (politics of belonging)" (p. 645). As Antonsich defines it, there is an important distinction between the subjective experience of belonging as connectedness to a place, whether that is literally the educational institution or figuratively the educational or societal space as a negotiated space of subjectivity and identity, and the understanding of how belonging to a place is defined by power structures such as hegemonic discourses about who has the right to claim the feeling of belonging. As Antonsich writes about feeling at home, it "stands for a symbolic space of familiarity, comfort, security, and emotional attachment" (Antonsich, 2010, p. 646) that educational institutions demarcate through both institutional criteria for selection and more subtle processes of cultural and psychosocial forms of sorting in the educational field and battle over cultural capital (Bourdieu, 1998). But in relation to a student life that intersects with education as dynamics of institutional and social sorting (Domina et al., 2017; Jørgensen, 2018), what Antonsich calls a contested discursive resource, accessibility to the phenomenological feeling of belonging, evolves within complex processes of power that can be found in the social-spatial forces of producing demarcated lines of inclusion and exclusion (Antonsich, 2010, p. 645). This entails an understanding of power in a differentiated manner. Holloway and Hubbard (2001), for instance, distinguish between power at a state level, such as surveillance, regulation and control, and power at a subjective level, such as self-regulation based on a self-monitoring of behaviour in accordance with a perception of something desirable or proper. Within educational institutions, this concerns power and the laws, regulation and regulations that determine formal criteria for accessibility and power as negotiated, where individuals can oppose and stand up to rulings as to what is stated as right and wrong (Holloway & Hubbard, 2001, p. 207).

But working across interviews and site visits was also an exercise that involved a desire to transcend the literal educational space as the primary space of sense-making in relation to experiences of psychological problems and life as a student. It was around these and other theoretical strands (see Chapter 1) that we went from thick descriptions into a mode of thematic analysis, trying to represent different understandings of how a life as a student with psychosocial problems appears when battling for belonging in Danish higher education. After each round of interviews and site visits, the empirical data were analysed and the overarching themes enumerated. As we gradually gained a longitudinal perspective on each student, other patterns emerged that added to the complexity of the findings. The research process was a continual hermeneutic process going from parts to whole and back, through iterations of dialogue and discussion and with the research group members challenging each other at each step of the process. As the group consisted of educational researchers with different academic backgrounds from the social sciences and humanities, and a range of professional interests, functions and experiences, the different perspectives and contributions were of great benefit in the iterations of the analysis in the search to understand the complexity and reach complex explanations.

References

Åkerström, J., & Brunnberg, E. (2013). Young people as partners in research: Experiences from an interactive research circle with adolescent girls. *Qualitative Research*, *13*(5), 528–545.

Alheit, P. (2012). Biografisk læring – inden for den nye diskurs om livslang læring. In K. Illeris (Ed.), *49 tekster om læring*. Samfundslitteratur.

Antonsich, M. (2010). Searching for belonging – an analytical framework. *Geography Compass*, *4*(6), 644–659.

Beresford, P. (2002). Thinking about 'mental health': Towards a social model. *Journal of Mental Health*, *11*(6), 581–584.

Biesta, G. (2009). Good education in an age of measurement: on the need to reconnect with the question of purpose in education. *Educational Assessment, Evaluation and Accountability*, *21*, 33–46. https://doi.org/10.1007/s11092-008-9064-9

Bourdieu, P. (1998). *Practical reason – on the theory of action*. Polity Press.

Burke, P. J., & Crozier, G. (2014). Higher education pedagogies: Gendered formations, mis/recognition and emotion. *Journal of Research in Gender Studies, 4*(2), 52–67.

Carspecken, F. P. (1996). *Critical ethnography in educational research: A Theoretical and practical guide*. Routledge.

Davies, B. (2000). *A body of writing 1990–1999*. Alta Mira Press.

Davies, B. (2014). *Listening to children: Being and becoming*. Routledge.

Denzin, N. K. (2018). *Performance autoethnography: Critical pedagogy and the politics of culture* (2nd ed.). Routledge. https://doi.org.ep.fjernadgang.kb.dk/10.4324/9781315159270

Domina, T., Penner, A., & Penner, E. (2017). Categorical inequality: Schools as sorting machines. *Annual Review of Sociology, 43*, 311–330.

Fraser, N. (2001). Recognition without ethics? *Theory, Culture & Society, 18*(2–3), 21–42.

Fraser, N. (2008). Fra omfordeling til anerkendelse? Retfærdighedens dilemmaer i en 'postsocialistisk' tidsalder. In M. H. Jacobsen & R. Willig (Eds.), *Anerkendelsespolitik* (pp. 58–93). Syddansk Universitetsforlag.

Freire, P. (1970). *Pedagogy of oppressed*. The Continuum International Publishing Group Inc.

Geertz, C. (1973). Thick description: Toward an interpretive theory of culture. *The interpretation of cultures: Selected essays* (pp. 3–30). Basic Books.

Harper, D. (2012). *Visual sociology*. Routledge.

Holloway, L., & Hubbard, P. (2001). *People and place: The extraordinary geographies of everyday life*. Pearson Education Limited.

Honneth, A. (1996). *The struggle for recognition – the moral grammar of social conflicts*. Polity Press.

Howard, L. C., & Ali, A. I. (2016). (Critical) educational ethnography: Methodological premise and pedagogical objectives. In A. Kaul & W. Rodick (Eds.), *New directions in educational ethnography: Shifts, problems, and reconstruction*. Emerald Publishing Limited.

Jørgensen, C. H. (2018). Inklusion i erhvervsuddannelse: Institutionel selektion og eksklusion i elevfællesskaber [Inclusion in vocational education: Institutional selection and exclusion in student communities]. In S. Baagøe Nielsen, S. Hvid Thingstrup, M. Brodersen, & H. Hersom (Eds.), *Drenge og mænds inklusion på kønnede uddannelser – erfaringer fra deltagerorienteret uddannelsesudvikling og – forskning i praksis* (pp. 61–84). Frydenlund Academic.

Lather, P. (2001). Postmodernism, post-structuralism and post(critical) ethnography: Of ruins, aporias and angels. In P. Atkinson, A. Coffey, S. Delamont, J. Lofland, & L. Lofland (Eds.), *Handbook of ethnography*. Sage Publications, Inc.

Madison, D. S. (2005). *Critical ethnography: Method, ethics, and performance*. Sage Publications, Inc.

Massey, D. (1994). *Space, place and gender*. Polity Press.

Morrow, V. (2008). Ethical dilemmas in research with children and young people about their social environments. *Children's Geographies, 6*(1), 49–61.

Rasmussen, K. (Ed.) (2013). *Visuelle tilgange og metoder i tværfaglige pædagogiske studier* [*Visual approaches and methods in interdisciplinary educational programmes*]. Roskilde Universitetsforlag.

Rasmussen, K. (2017). Photovoice. In J. Kampmann, K. Rasmussen, & H. Warming (Eds.), *Interview med børn* [*Interviews with children*] (pp. 127–146). Hans Reitzels Forlag.

Rinaldi, C. (2006). *In dialogue with Reggio Emilia: Listening, researching and learning*. Routledge.
Smith, D. E. (1989). *The everyday world as problematic*. Northeastern University Press.
Smith, D. E. (2005). *Institutional ethnography: A sociology for people*. AltaMira Press.
Smith, D. E. (2008). From the 14th floor to the sidewalk: Writing sociology at ground level. *Sociological Inquiry*, *78*(3), 417–422.
Spradly, J. P. (1979). *The ethnographic interview*. Wadsworth Group/Thomson Learning.
Storrie, K., Ahern, K., & Tuckett, A. (2010). A systematic review: Students with mental health problems – a growing problem. *International Journal of Nursing Practice*, *16*, 1–6.
Szulewicz, T. (2015). Deltagerobservation [Participant observation]. In S. Brinkmann & L. Tanggaard (Eds.), *Kvalitative metoder – en grundbog [Qualitative methods: A basic textbook]* (2nd ed.). Hans Reitzels Forlag.
Thomas, J. (1993). *Doing critical ethnography*. Sage Publications, Inc.
Titchkosky, T. (2011). *The question of access: Disability, space, meaning*. University of Toronto Press.
Wenger, E. (1998). *Communities of practice: Learning, meaning, and identity*. Cambridge University Press.
Wengraf, T. (2001). *Qualitative research interviewing: Biographic narratives and semi-structured methods*. Sage Publications, Inc.
Willis, P. (1978). *Learning to labour – how working class kids get working class jobs*. Ashgate Publishing Group.
Wulf-Andersen, T. Ø., Follesø, R., & Olsen, T. (2021). *Involving methods in youth research: Reflections on participation and power*. Palgrave-Macmillan.
Wulf-Andersen, T. Ø., & Neidel, A. V. (2012). The ethics of involvement with the already involved: Action research and power. In L. Phillips, M. Kristiansen, M. Vehviläinen, & E. Gunnarson (Eds.), *Knowledge and power in collaborative research: A reflexive approach* (pp. 153–170). Routledge.

4 "If I look at myself . . ." Poetic representations of students' negotiations of self

In this chapter, we present a series of poetic representations of students' understandings and (re)presentations of themselves (Görlich, 2016; Wulf-Andersen, 2012). The poetic representations are developed on the basis of the overall research problem of the book, namely battling, belonging and recognition, but with a focus on representing the experiences and learning processes that stem from struggles with feeling at home in higher education and society alike.

With the employment of literary or poetic elements in the social sciences, different poststructuralist-inspired feminist traditions have sought to unfold and explore sensory dimensions of research representation (Görlich, 2016; Hulgård Kristiansen, 2022, forthcoming; Krøjer, 2003; Lawrence-Lightfoot & Davis, 1997; Wulf-Andersen, 2012). A shared ambition is to involve the reader, to make the reader feel and understand the position of research subjects as well as the limitations of patriarchal sociology (Richardson, 1993), in which the scientific criteria leave little space for research subjects to inspire others and define what is important in their lives, and hence should be important for research. In this sense, these efforts resemble the critique behind critical ethnography as well as the development of institutional ethnography as a 'sociology for people' (Carroll, 2011; Madison, 2004; Smith, 2005, 2006).

Working from the theoretical and ethical imperative of the student perspective, as argued in Chapter 3, is not a simple question of giving priority to student voices in the data. Rather, it denotes the exploration of ways to represent the complexity of students' situated experiential standpoint – what it is like when 'you are here' (Hulgård Kristiansen, 2022, forthcoming) – as important contributions to our understanding of and theorizing about higher education (cf. James, 2007). Exploring performative ways to write goes beyond a matter of merely representing. As stated by art philosopher Susanne Langer (1953), attempts to describe emotions also belong in the non-discursive domain, since experiences of emotions can only with difficulty and short circuits be described with direct translation. Instead of attempts to translate an emotional state with precision, performative forms of writing always leave something for the reader to interpret, which has to be sensed or felt by the reader. This becomes difficult with the language of science adhering to rational explanation and interpretation. Rather, emotional experiences originating in complex psychosocial problems represent

DOI: 10.4324/9781003221029-4

themselves as attached to organic, mental and emotional states of experiences that contain more than a standard scientific linguistic representation can capture (Langer, 1953, pp. 240–241)

Providing poetic representations to disturb the dominant voice and genre of researchers such as ourselves, and promoting student experience and sensory and emotional dimensions, stems from an overarching ambition of solidarity with student perspectives. But poetic representations must also be recognized as a non-innocent involvement in a non-innocent space (Lather, 2007). This calls for transparency and reflexivity regarding the positions and power relations proposed by research questions, research design and research relationships as discussed in Chapter 3, and we should expect the same kind of reflexivity regarding the (forms of) representation presented in research publications (Wulf-Andersen et al., 2021). There is always a risk of glossing over the ways in which we are involved in higher education, not only as researchers but also as teachers, supervisors, heads of programmes and other powerful actors.

The strength of poetic analysis is that it allows plural perspectives or voices to be present(ed) at the same time (Görlich, 2016). One voice is the voice of the student, that is, the scenes, words and metaphors, the pauses and rhythms and nuances of the student's story. Another voice is the voice of the researcher, contributing his/her questions to what is included and explored in the student's story in the first place and what is selected for closer analysis. Integrated in this voice is a third voice of theory, the epistemology and concepts guiding the analysis and production of the poetic representations (Görlich, 2016; Hulgård Kristiansen, 2022, forthcoming). All three voices are present in the poetic representations, when the text encounters a fourth party in the dialogue with the reader (Smith, 2005).

Poetic representations were created after the analysis of transcripts and observational notes from the interviews and visits with a particular student. In this analysis and development of the poems, we have given priority to the ambivalences characterizing students' self-reflection and self-negotiation, their battling for recognition and belonging and their learning processes with their ever-changing perspectives on themselves in their own eyes or in the eyes of imagined others. We selected passages where students literally or metaphorically describe or characterize themselves (or their process) as students in higher education related to their struggle for belonging or the ways they try to adapt or work on themselves to fit into higher education. These passages have also been condensed, where we cut out words or sentences and reconstruct them into shorter quotes, representing central motifs, ambivalences or insights in the particular student's story. These steps resemble the analytical process of writing up more classic chronological prose portraits, "so frequently used in ethnographic research that it seems almost neutral" (Wulf-Andersen, 2012, p. 568). Poetic representations, however, in their composition and graphical arrangement look like poems, slowing down the reader's pace (Wulf-Andersen, 2012).

Poetic representations provide a kind of condensed yet open-ended analysis and a textual representation of research results close to the nuances, ambivalences and inconsistencies, as well as storylines and themes, in the students' narratives and in the researchers' interpretations without finalizing the possible interpretations. Working analytically through an emphasis on poetic, aesthetic use of language can include and impress the reader with a sensoriality often absent in research publications, by showing rather than explaining student experience (Wulf-Andersen, 2012, p. 573). It evokes sentiments and emotional responses in the reader by staying close to the immediate words and multiple layers of meaning-making in students' propositions and understandings of themselves. In this sense, it provides an analysis more open-ended than traditional academic analyses such as the ones we will proceed with in the following chapters.

"If I look at myself..."

Not really there (Vera)

You're sitting in a train
everything is sort of going past
you're not really there

The days just go by
you think
you're doing
what you're supposed to
I feel like
I'm not really there

Could be a lack of energy
maybe the wrong idea about energy
I'm sure I'd have more energy
if I
started exercising
went to a psychologist
learned to set limits

I dip in icy water
that might reset my system
if I've been stressed
I do lots of things with my flat
alone
it becomes my outer skin

I went to the doctor
to take a test, get a diagnosis
there are some blinking warning
 lights there

I'm way too conscious of myself

Sometimes it feels like
everything's just a play
I walk around this town
looking at people
I look at my flat
and think:
Is this where I live?

Got in on my third choice
got a chance, took it
failed, was on sick leave
postponed my dream for a year

Now finally I feel like
I'm really here
But it still seems like I'm in a play

Today I was waiting at the bus stop
all my thoughts
are something like:
wonder what the others are thinking
 about me?
do they think I'm in control?
how does my make-up look?

I'd really do a lot
just to be able to stay
in my very own world
just lie about in it
really be there

Me as a student (Alexander)

Me as a student?

Can I just go to the toilet
and I'll think a bit about it

what's it called again,
that myth in Greek mythology
Siphys? Syphises?
arrggh . . .
that's exactly the image
the best metaphor for studying

you get the rock to the top
you really struggle
it gets steeper and steeper
the higher up you get

then exam comes
you finish it
and you let go of the rock
you go back down again
and again
a constant battle
you keep at it
on and on

it feels like an eternity
you struggle
keep at it
Even in situations
where you've just had enough
where you get tired of everything
    around you
where you've failed the exam
you try again

an unrewarding eternal battle

The good student (Jenny)

The general idea
of a good student
is someone who
gets all her stuff done
shows up at all lectures
can handle the syllabus
can almost answer things
before she's even learnt them

my idea
that is
to handle the syllabus as well as I can
to realize more realistically
that you can't manage all of it,
a balance between spare time and
    studies
so you don't get burnt out

it's ok how you study
what your learning process is
it's not the same for everybody

there's this idea
of what a good student is
every lecture you go to
it's like the teachers
have a sort of idea
that we know it all
and we've learnt a whole lot
already
so we'll grasp everything at once

It can easily feel
like a race
to be quickest, first
and best,
it creates pressure
people start competing

I think that's why
you think
"they're in control"
"she's a good student"
"they do all their stuff,
hand in all their work"

but the more you ask people
the more reality is quite different

several of them tell me
they can't hand in all the work
there's not always time to read
    everything
and write all the essays

But I just have a feeling
it's still all about
doing those things
to be a good student

In control (Sofie)

It's not often
I go home in time
it's all about balance

if I want to go to class
I have to pay that bill
for ever weighing things up in my mind
need to catch up on that subject
been off sick
in a new class for the third time
sticking out

so there I sit
radiating
a kind of calm
mainly because I'm paralyzed
it looks like
I'm in control
of everything

I hate dressing up (Dea)

If I look at myself from the outside
I'm really not stable
things change for me

I can't assume
that the big picture will be stable
but I can build structure
into my everyday life

it's not that I'm afraid
of doing something that's not right
of stepping out of line
it's not uncertainty about my subject

I become existentially insecure
if I have to do something
I don't quite understand

I always wear the same clothes
the only difference is long trousers or shorts
winter boots or summer shoes
a woollen jumper over the shirt
I always wear underneath

I'm not myself
if I'm wearing other clothes
I hate dressing up
it makes me a different person

some people are always dressing up
like it gives them a sense of freedom
"now that'll be fun"
"now I can pretend I'm in another role"
"a different identity for an evening"

it's really awful
I hate it
social rules and norms
conventions
if I mix in with the crowd
I lose myself

when that happens
I run away
Escape from the room

One thing a day I can do (Laura)

I used to be very sociable
But it just takes too much out of you

I have one thing a day I can do
today the thing is that you're coming

pain every day
my energy production down 60–70%
tired
my senses are more intense
sensitive to sounds and light
stomach cramps
burning pain in the back of my head
it's changed my whole life

I don't look ill

Tomorrow I'll be studying
for my next lecture
One thing a day I can do

can't ask for a note
from my doctor
she knows nothing about this

there's a whole lot
that diverts my attention
from just being at the uni
listening to the lecture and taking part

it's a paradox
that I have to spend so much energy
on taking a break

I walk in the opposite direction
from the others
I go the other way
to get peace in my head
with noise cancelling headphones
it seems antisocial
I had to tell them,
"It's got nothing to do with you"

I don't look ill
It would show
if I had chemotherapy

got an examination at the hospital
can't move the appointment
for lots of the lectures
attendance is compulsory
I'll miss two
when I'm at the hospital
I can't have a bad day

One thing a day I can do
if I can manage till 12 o'clock
I'll go straight home to sleep

if I haven't studied for a class
I've felt awful
it can easily look like
I'm not taking it seriously
using it as an excuse

I recently tried to swap two subjects
that's really difficult
I think it's a principle
I've read somewhere
that they want to treat all students equally
they can see my excellent marks
If it was up to me
I'd take one course less

I've attached a picture
pink roses
that ALWAYS bloom
the whole year
in the darkest darkness
something fresh, beautiful and luxuriant
they bloom in spite of everything
and give hope

I have one thing a day I can do

"If I look at myself..."

A memoir to myself (Jamie)

small town
small family
my old school

school was a shadow
took two years off, down in a depression
nothing really happened
didn't really eat anything
no normal sleeping times
the same town, no normal sleep
staying up till four in the morning
sleeping for twelve hours

the army was fantastic
clear structure
clear tracks to follow
it's easier to change yourself
when you change the context
maybe I should just pull myself together?

business junior consultant
e-mails at 10.30 p.m.
compliments for replying

a memoir to myself
get going
show your worth
in control
achievement
deep water

absent-minded
more golf
later to bed
more work
caffeine pills
nosebleed and headaches
cracked nails
losing hair
gum infection
bleeding

a memoir to myself
show your worth
please
get going
fear of getting stuck

Muddled and murky (Esther)

A strange murky picture
I'm a strange person

it was natural for me to do my master's
in terms of my interests, my level
however
it's just been one hell of a mess

especially my sisters
and my parents
thought and said at times
        "shouldn't you just give it up?
          give it up now,
          give it up now"
they thought it was too hard

I was offended,
felt they were suggesting I couldn't work it out

I've got two sisters
almost the same age as me
they go to the uni and . . .

I thought
I felt
I feel
at home in that way of studying

there might have been a programme
more suitable
to my challenges
there may well have been one.
I don't know.

I don't think
my problems will go away
if I study elsewhere

My cheering squad (Beate)

My mentor and my advisor
my cheering squad
like if you think about
good things
your mother's told you
they know what
who I really am
they know the battle
I'm having on the side

Straight-A student (Jamie)

Full-time studies
that's not enough
you need to do more
unless you're a complete straight-A pupil
or have a defect
you must be lazy

straight-A student
I filled my calendar
lectures
networking groups

I'm sure
my CV looks good
compared to others

If you can start with a sun (Beate)

if you can start with a sun
you can finish with a black cloud

Being talked down to (Eva)

I can't really know
if it's especially me

I do have my baggage
my history
mentally vulnerable
or something

There's a teacher
I want to ask about something
then she stares at me
           'aren't you supposed to have almost graduated?'
indirectly:
           'you must be an idiot, asking like that.'

if I didn't have all these mental problems
I'd probably be better
and I'd wish I knew all these things
I might have taken some course
so I could handle it

but being talked down to
there's no real science that says
if you talk down to people
it makes them better

Huge progress (Jenny)

There has been huge progress
for me
in what I can do
I wouldn't have believed it
but I'm glad I'm able to do it
to continue

there has been *huge* progress
is it ok to say that I'm the main reason for it?
well, I think so

it's still hard
it's just something I really want to do
so there's no possibility of giving up
saying 'I've had enough of this'

I'll have to see
I've found out what didn't work
where I needed to work on some things
getting better at having good study habits
finding out
that I work in a different way from other students
and that's quite okay
realizing I'm responsible
for my own studies
for getting where I want to be
I just have to keep trying
as best I can
and it has
actually
turned out
very well

It's hard for me to be with a lot of people
sit in a big lecture hall
group work
lots of people
lots of people talking at the same time
hard for me to concentrate
need a quieter environment
need to ask for help

you can write to the teaching assistants
and I've started to ask other students
but I prefer to try myself first
if I can't quite figure out
how to solve this problem
then I'll ask for help

A bad chameleon (Beate)

A buffet
I can decide
what to eat

I try to sort it a bit
could eat it all at one go
if it's too popular
everyone would want it
find something unique

I reckon the things and people around me decide
what I can and can't do

I don't blend in
I'm not a very invisible student
I'm very active
I'd actually like to be invisible

It's a bad chameleon
that can't find out
how to blend in

Those two girls (Louise)

> I tend to stay in my seat
> those thoughts could come back to me
> keep me stuck in the situation
> it's unpleasant
> uncertain
>
> what shall I do?
> who shall I talk to?
> maybe I shouldn't talk to anyone?
>
> my body reacts
> my hands get quite cold
> I clench my teeth
> feel cold all over
> despite my three layers of clothes
> I'm still feeling cold sitting here
> headache and dizziness
> can't concentrate
>
> one of the subjects
> where I'd be with those two girls
> I decided to postpone it
> I couldn't stand it
> I'll be six months behind
> but it was the best thing for me to do

The big difference (Christine)

The really big difference
between higher education
and all other education
is that the teachers don't know who you are

one teacher
I really liked a lot
told me I could call her in the evenings
we had good talks
once I cried when I called her

after the exam
I went up to her to say hello
she couldn't remember me

Battle with all I've got (Alicia)

A person lying in water up to her nose
splashes with her arms

I'll splash and thrash about
battle with all I've got
there's only one person to make sure I do it
and that's me

the feeling of being helpless
anxiety right into, far into my bones
knowing that only one person can do something
and that's you
and you've got no strength left

Wired up differently (Oscar)

It's all about doing
the right things
at the right times
– even if you don't want to
It's all about
having a brain
that's wired up differently

It's a lot more difficult
to get down to work yourself
Others think
'oh yes, I can do that'
I can sometimes join in
when we're here studying
when I get home
things look quite different
I'm in charge now
and that's a huge problem for me

When I get home
I'm usually tired
it kind of depends on
whether I've taken Ritalin
because that's what I take
When I come home from the uni,
I usually need to lie down
for a bit
do something quite different
then it's hard to get started
on my home assignment

Shall I go to bed
when I feel best?
It's completely quiet
I can relax
I'm not stressed
no anxiety
or negative thoughts
it's a quiet time
in the evening
when it's dark
and ten-eleven-twelve o'clock
I know others are asleep
I'm sitting here
and hell, do I feel great
just now

I have an inner feeling
created from things inside myself
not created from things
brought in
it may seem antisocial
maybe I'm exaggerating
but that's the feeling

I've got better at it
stopped playing computer games a lot
I still play a bit
but that's acceptable
now and then
but it's not at a harmful level

now I just need to find out
how to use my spare time
to do something sensible
instead of just sitting
doing stupid things

Not enough nerds (Beate)

    I haven't had any study group
    on this master's course
    I've been very alone
    you really are very alone
    when you have no other students
    when you don't have a regular group
    like I was used to

    there are lots of things
    to talk about in religion
    but there are simply not enough students
    who feel like it
    there aren't enough nerds

Forever in my head (Aron)

It's forever in my head
go out and find a job
you must find a job
you mustn't be someone
who waits half a year before getting a job
don't be a lazy foreigner
a lazy student
a lazy father
a lazy lover
a bad lover
you need money
for a good life
I'll do whatever I can

My first visit to a psychologist they said
you have a stress disorder
you've pushed yourself too hard
I'm depressed
I'm stressed
I have anxiety
I have PTSD
because of my life history

Two poles (Dea)

Wavering
a long, long way between two poles
nothing in between
one or the other

studying, studying, studying, studying
passing all my exams
with an A and even more
or
nothing

extremely studious and conscientious
and drained of energy
just be a university student
nothing else
or
won't touch it with a bargepole

I'm approaching a mid-point
my awful physical condition forces me
to find a middle way

Every cloud has a silver lining

Things may turn out well again (Ida)

I've become a changed person
because of my studies
because of my therapy

you may well change things . . .
but I'm not quite sure
if you can

Part of the baggage
I'm stuck with
it makes me stand out
I'm older than the others

there have been big changes in
what I thought
I could be
From having no idea
that I could be anything at all
I started on a path
Things may turn out well again
I just have to hand in this exam

My life as a student (Kenneth)

A duck pond
lots of activity
but on the wrong track
species out of balance
too much seaweed, too much algae
the algae have got too big
everything's got too murky
I've seen very dark, gloomy periods in my life

the algae, the dregs
it's not clear enough to find the big fish
the big fish as in wisdom or learning
it's been hard for me to find my way to them

it wasn't until recently
I noticed the big fish
in the duck pond

or in the river
a big river might be a better symbol
a river where things sort of
come and go

there's now a certain clarity
the algae have been cleared out
the fish suddenly came to me
and I learned something important about myself

References

Görlich, A. (2016). Afstand, modstand og mestring: Poetiske analyser af unges subjektiveringsprocesser [Distance, resistance and mastery: Poetic analyses of young people's subjectivization processes]. *Psyke & Logos, 37*(1), 225–247.

Krøjer, J. (2003). *Det mærkede sted: Køn, krop og arbejdsrelationer* [*The marked place: Gender, body and work relationships*]. Graduate School in Lifelong Learning, Roskilde University Press.

Langer, K. S. (1953). *Feeling and form. A theory of art*. Charles Scribner's Sons.

Lather, P. (2000). Against empathy, voice and authenticity. *Kvinder, køn og forskning, 9*(4), 16–25.

Lather, P., & Smithies, C. (1997). *Troubling the angels: Women living with HIV/AIDS*. Westview Press.

Lawrence-Lightfoot, S. (2005). Reflections on portraiture: A dialogue between art and science. *Qualitative Inquiry, 11*(1), 3–15. https://doi.org/10.1177/1077800404270955

Lawrence-Lightfoot, S., & Davis, J. H. (1997). *The art and science of portraiture*. Jossey-Bass.

Smith, D. E. (2005). *Institutional ethnography: A sociology for people*. AltaMira Press.

Smith, D. E. (Ed.). (2006). *Institutional ethnography as practice*. Rowman & Littlefield.

Wulf-Andersen, T. (2012). Poetic representation: Working with dilemmas of involvement in participative social work research. *European Journal of Social Work, 15*(4), 563–580. https://doi.org/10.1080/13691457.2012.705261

Wulf-Andersen, T., Warming, H., & Neidel, A. (2021). Power and reflexivity: Positions and positioning in involving research with young people. In T. Wulf-Andersen, R. Follesø, & T. Olsen (Eds.), *Involving methods in youth research: Reflections on participation and power* (pp. 17–46). Palgrave Macmillan.

5 "Like everyone else can." Shameful identities and the narrative of the 'good student' in higher education

> *In our society, there's so much focus on getting an education and getting on with it, and if you do it quickly, it is as though you score more points or something. So in some corner of the subconscious, there's a realisation that it must be all wrong if I can't complete a study programme, like everyone else can.*

Alicia did not complete the first study programme she took in higher education. In the quote above, she expresses how a constant presence of an intense societal expectation regarding young people and education might influence students who do not move smoothly through education: the impression from public discourse and local study cultures that 'everyone else can' made Alicia feel 'all wrong' when she could not. She describes her experience of that period of her life as 'suffering through education' and as a time with 'lots of guilt and shame.'

In our research project, we have been struck by the frequency and the intensity with which students have talked about shame, felt ashamed of themselves and battled with their sense of (academic) self-identity and self-worth. Students experiencing psychosocial problems often (come to) understand themselves as less worthy or unworthy students, an understanding that undermines their sense of belonging in higher education.

In this chapter, we explore three students' experiences of shame in relation to higher education and their local study cultures. The examples of Alicia, Molly and Signe show how shame relates to different aspects of higher education. To Alicia, the overriding shame issue relates to understanding the ways of higher education and to finding her place and sense of belonging in the learning community. To Molly, shame relates to working and writing practices. To Signe, shame relates to dilemmas of getting support and positioning herself as a competent and ambitious student.

We take the three students' stories as exemplary entry points for exploring which normative ideas of the 'good student' are reference points in students' ongoing negotiations of themselves as students. Understanding shame as an emotional experience of being 'wrong' or 'in opposition to' what one is supposed to be as a student and exploring the situations and contexts of shameful experience can help us understand the expectations and images of the 'good student,' which

DOI: 10.4324/9781003221029-5

students find in particular educational contexts. We analyse how the emotional experience of shame intertwines with normative ideas of individual work routines and independently working students. We argue that these normative ideas intersect with broader dilemmas of disclosure of psychosocial problems and dilemmas for students who not only need support but also want to make themselves visible as competent students. Inspired by Burke and Crozier's analyses of the formation of 'proper students' (2014), and Skeggs's concept of 'person value' (Skeggs, 1997; Loveday, 2016), we show how students' (educational and personal) biographies, educational cultures and societal contexts interweave in their continual negotiations of and inner dialogues on their own value and 'proper' or 'suitable' student identities (Burke & Crozier, 2014; Skeggs, 2011).

Shame and becoming in higher education

Central to the analysis of shame in higher education is the question of what is explicitly or implicitly, formally or informally, held as the standard when students (with psychosocial problems) are valued and value themselves. Burke (2012) and Burke and Crozier (2014) point out that in spite of discourses of widening participation in higher education, the challenges of participation of diverse student groups have not attracted sufficient attention, and there has been too little focus on how current forms of support might actually be exclusive through standardizing and homogenizing practices:

> *The forms of support provided in universities tend to be remedial in nature, designed to re/form those students identified as 'non-standard' into legitimate, normalized subjects. This requires the 'non-standard student' to participate in processes of self-transformation and self-regulation, to become a 'proper' university student, fitting in to the dominant culture and framework.*
> (Burke & Crozier, 2014, p. 54)

We analyse shame as experiences of contested belonging, as a symptom of misrecognition, in the sense that it points to cultural and institutionalized interpretations and evaluations, constituting some students as non-standard and not (yet) proper. We are interested in shame as experiences that address the ideas and values of 'good students,' contributing to the subtle positioning of some subjects as comparatively unworthy of respect or esteem, essentially denying them status and participation as peers (cf. Fraser in Frost, 2016, p. 432). We thus analyse students' experiences of shame not just as intrapersonal or interpersonal but as inextricably linked to dominant cultures, structural powers, educational discourses and local communities that define some subjects as 'good' or 'proper' and others as 'unworthy.' Alicia's feeling of shame and of being 'all wrong' signals the state of the relationship or bond between the individual and society as somehow threatened or disconnected (Scheff, 2014, p. 133). Our analysis focuses on students' sense of shame and threatened belonging in higher education in relation to psychosocial problems. But issues of class, gender and culture certainly intersect with the definitions of psychosocial problems in the inscription of lack of value, pathologization and the naturalization of deficiencies in the representation of particular students. Theoretically, we are inspired by authors who have analysed shame as an important dimension of the lived experience of (staff and) students of working-class background in English higher education institutions (Skeggs, 1997; Jimenez & Walkerdine, 2011; Loveday, 2016) and by authors who approach shame from a gender perspective (Burke & Crozier, 2014).

Structural relations, cultural and institutional codes and social dynamics intertwine with students' personal, classed and gendered biographies, when students with particular backgrounds enter an educational field with established traditions and cultural values that connect to wider societal understandings of academic or occupational worthiness. Loveday (2016) theorizes on shame as a way to emphasize people's active engagement in and constitution through current and past practice. In her analysis, adopting Skeggs's notion of 'person value,' she describes how systems of inscription, valuing and institutionalization are reproduced by some groups at the expense of others, through practices of exclusion (Loveday, 2016, p. 1141). Inspired by this, we seek to address the complexity of student becoming (Colley et al., 2003). What makes students feel they are right or 'all wrong,' and suited or not to particular study programmes? How do students experience themselves as proper or unproper, worthy or unworthy, in the educational culture and social communities they seek to enter on their study programme? How does their sense of identity change, as they become, or do not become, recognized as a member of that community?

The students' experiences of shame show how domains of the social, cultural and emotional are integral dimensions of learning processes, not just "a set of external factors that may affect learning" (Colley et al., 2003, p. 473). When students experience shame, all these dimensions are involved in a process of *learning as becoming*: a process of orientation and identity work containing "important contradictory tensions, which the learner must negotiate" (Colley et al., 2003, p. 489). This kind of identity work involves students' framing and narrating their background, individual preferences and life experiences as part of what leads or predisposes them to be(come) 'right for the job,' right for the study programme, right for the community. This includes the continual (re)construction of failures, difficulties, overcomings and successes as positive, or even constitutive, related to idealized images of being 'proper' or 'suitable,' mediated by educational institutions and learning cultures (Colley et al., 2003, pp. 488–489). Educational institutions and settings thus play a powerful role in the social and cultural construction of a sense of 'suitability' for a certain type of knowledge, work and academic identity (Colley et al., 2003, p. 477) of oneself as a 'proper student.' Our argument is that subtle sorting processes (Larsen et al., 2020; Brown, 2018; Soldatic & Morgan, 2017) are complicit in student shame processes and that student shame processes are in themselves symptoms of inequality and central to the inertia of widening participation in higher education (cf. Thomsen, 2021).

However, the experience of shame often misrepresents the problem as the property, characteristic or (dis)ability of individuals and the project as one of subjects' self-correction (Burke & Crozier, 2014, p. 56). Accordingly, students might experience shame as "an intense feeling of the subject 'being against itself'" (Burke, 2017, p. 435). Rather than leading to a focus on "the social structures, discourses and practices, entangled in the politics of misrecognition" (Burke, 2017, p. 435), an inherently social problem is "easily . . . turned into a deficiency of the self" (Loveday, 2016, p. 1143). Hence, there is a need for our analysis to highlight the social, cultural and structural dimensions of the problems, and the particular ways students relate or translate problems to properties of the self. In other words, we explore how students experience institutionalized patterns, categorizations and inscriptions as seeping into them, and how they "come to believe this story of inadequacy themselves" (Loveday, 2016, pp. 1145–1146).

'Feeling wrong': struggling to decode Law School

On entering higher education, Alicia had "picture-perfect" ideas of "who I'd like to be, how it would be to study and live in the city." A lawyer at the law firm where she worked encouraged Alicia to apply for Law School. Being the first one from her family to enter higher education[1], Alicia was flattered and proud of the suggestion and later of the fact that she was accepted. She moved into her own flat, expecting the kind of life she had when working in the law firm. However, when she started at Law School, "all that was gone. I didn't work there any more, I didn't have those colleagues, and I'd moved away from home and was in this flat which was just completely empty." From early on, Alicia felt alone, and things at Law School were not what she had expected. For various reasons, all the other students in Alicia's study group dropped out very early in the term, and no measures were taken to help Alicia into another group. Where other students had support from the group in remembering instructions, registering for exams, looking through the curriculum, etc., Alicia felt she was hanging by a thread, having more and more difficulty in coping. She says:

> *After a while, I became more and more anxious about showing up, because I was imagining the others thinking, "What the hell is she doing here, that idiot, why hasn't she given up yet?" – and then I just sort of ended up staying home around the clock, without having anything to do, other than sitting and reading those chapters, over and over and over again, and then turning up to the exam and failing everything on the first try, every time.*

Without a study group as a forum for feedback and discussion, Alicia had difficulty in working out how to move forward and improve academically. Her family had no experience with higher education, so it was hard to use them for reflection and developing strategies. She says:

> *I remember my father was outraged, because it's higher education, it's a university, but he was like "This can't be right, they tell you you've made all these mistakes in the paper, but you're not told what the mistakes are – and then you're*

supposed to improve on this next time" . . . *"But Dad, they can't do that for everybody, do you realize how many people there are, at a university like that? And one lecturer for over 200 students, you just can't do that"*

Alicia at the time (more readily than her father) accepted the premise, that guidance, feedback and questions were not common or possible at the university. Feedback is not a simple need to correct specific errors. Without dialogue with fellow students and teachers, or with her family, there was no one to seek advice from, and it became increasingly difficult for Alicia to explore and understand in a broad sense what is valued and appreciated academically, how she could find a forum for collective reflection, and essentially how she could transform a difficult experience into learning or criticism. Alicia directed the criticism towards herself: she should have been able to manage this by herself.

The atmosphere at Law School was generally very competitive and prestige-oriented and did not encourage questions from students even in smaller classes. Students looked down upon those with poor marks or no student job in a law firm, which were valuation criteria emphasized formally and by staff at Law School. Appearances and expensive clothes, bags and jewellery seemed very important as status symbols. Alicia could not afford to keep up with this, and felt "embarrassed" to be "flat broke":

> *I can remember what it was like, that you just didn't . . . you went around looking for those damn bottles and people who dropped money on the ground and so on . . . and I can remember how awful that was, how embarrassed you were to ask if you could borrow some money.*

Alicia describes a humiliating incident from the lecture hall, when she observed a student who asked if she could sit next to another student, but ended up sitting on the floor, because the other student "wasn't prepared to move her Gucci bag from the seat, because the floor was sticky." To Alicia, student talk about other students was harsh rather than supportive:

> *What was talked about instead was more along the lines of –* "*This is completely ridiculous, I mean, why is he even here. . . . Just think of all the other students who wanted to get in to this course*" *– you know, in a way it started to be a bit judgmental. And I remember being told that there was a bloke from my own class who said that about me, to a mutual friend. Like, that was just, it made me even more ashamed and it was so depressing, and I started to feel even more embarrassed about showing up.*

Alicia felt worse and worse, having anxiety, stress and sleeping and eating problems. Nevertheless, she had a strong obligation to stay, to complete her education, and could not "just give up." As she says in the introductory quote: "it must be all wrong if I can't complete a study programme, like everyone else can."

Alicia's experience from Law School is a good example of a student 'feeling lost' in a study environment highly attuned to capitalist, competitive, neoliberal values. The public discourse in the media on dropout, and formal systems of rewarding fast track students, influences Alicia's valuation of her own performance. With these broad discourses and the local study culture as her mirror, the interpretation that problems are due to her own shortcomings or deficits seeps into Alicia, and she turns against herself (cf. Burke, 2017). Shame becomes a deeply bodily experience for Alicia. Importantly, controlling her weight becomes her way of complying with a culture of looks and control, and even 10 years later, remembering Law School in the interview makes her feel physically ill.

> *I've had the most extreme, most malicious inferiority complexes from seeing how all my old school friends, right after graduating with their master's degrees, they just sprouted wings and took off; and I was really happy for them, but wow did I feel wrong, and like "I don't belong in this society." Everyone is busy with their own things, and I'm just walking around in this bubble and thinking, like, I have no purpose.*

We see how Alicia describes the immediate link between structural damage, social relations and personal elements of well-being (Frost, 2016). The structural call for completed education as the way to demonstrate your worth, purpose and belonging in society sets the scene, where Alicia feels cut off from her social relations, left behind by her 'old school friends,' who graduate and 'take off.' On a personal level, she is overwhelmed with 'malicious inferiority' and 'feeling wrong.' With no sense of direction, 'I have no purpose,' Alicia in a sense experiences a loss of her right to participation in or membership of society, 'like I don't belong in this society.' Shame is the emotional term Alicia presents as a collective name for a range of feelings of being wrong, unworthy, without purpose, inferior, etc. Shame marks Alicia's (re)orientation in educational relations, cultures and contexts, not just as a responsive reaction in her attempt to adapt to demands for efficiency and performativity, but as an (inter)subjective experience shaping both Alicia's identity and self-understanding and the collective identity and cultural figures of higher education, of Law School.

Institutional traditions and values in different higher education settings shape the social valuation practices in the above-mentioned examples, thereby facilitating particular conditions for students' relations. Shame relates to valuation practices, which sometimes play out very explicitly and tangibly in exclusionary dynamics amongst students turning against each other (cf. Burke, 2017), like at Alicia's Law School. The (inadvertent) role of staff in preparing for particular cultures of dos/don'ts, and who is in/out, also seems very important. However, valuation also works through students' own regulation of themselves, when students turn against themselves. Both kinds of valuation and exclusion mechanisms affect students in the form of shame, seen by students as glaring personal deficits rather than 'disorders' of the context. The context here would also be broad societal exclusion dynamics. At Law School, students compete with themselves and with each other, preparing for a highly competitive vocational culture amongst lawyers and barristers. Inequality and exclusion working through shame are powerful in this way. It makes students hide and blame themselves. It preys on their sense of being a worthy or even a possible participant, not only in higher education but also in the world in a broad sense. In this way, shame discourages these students from expecting or believing in their own worthiness, belonging and feeling of community, and from thinking that they can have a place in society, up to the point where a student rather than a Gucci bag sits on the sticky floor.

Not having 'much to offer': struggling with individual(ized) work routines

As implied earlier, some of Alicia's blaming herself has to do with work routines. Many students in our project take work routines as a primary parameter for evaluating and valuing themselves as students. They lead ongoing negotiations with themselves on how students should work, how they themselves are able to work or not, and how failing to work in the right manner and the right amount of time might mean that they are lazy. On an everyday basis, students orient themselves and their study routines towards working long and hard, presenting themselves as capable, and completing what they started on time, compliant to neoliberal higher education. They thus have something to offer, being 'right' for the specific study programme.

Molly is a 30-year-old university student of international politics. Her experience with anxiety and depression began when she started her master's programme. In the beginning, she found it difficult to realize she was ill. She was ashamed of her situation, and for a long time she did not share it with anyone, not even her parents:

> *Well, I thought I was lazy, but somehow I also knew, it might not be that either, but . . . So for two months, I just lay in my bed every day and ate sweets and watched Netflix and I think when I finally decided not to hand in my work, to take leave . . . that lifted the weight off my shoulders a bit, and then actually I started exercising a lot instead (laughs).*

Initially, Molly was scared about what was happening to her, and explaining her situation in terms of laziness rather than illness made the situation somewhat less frightening but also more shameful. Shifting the understanding of her situation to that of illness with depression, Molly says, "I'm not going to die and I also know somehow that it's in my head what's going on now." After deciding to take leave, she felt much better, at least for a while, but since then, studying has been associated with shifting energy and constantly battling against feelings of defeat.

In particular, when Molly started on her master's thesis, problems arose and she felt a lot of pressure. One problem was that she could not write as fast and well as she felt expected to do:

> *I often have expectations of, well ok, tomorrow I'll get up at six o'clock and start writing, so if I haven't done that, then I thought like argh, now it's running a bit late, but maybe I can open my computer after dinner tonight.*

Molly entered a vicious circle, writing too little on her thesis and blaming herself, which made her concentration on writing even worse. Molly had both paid work and voluntary work, which helped her not only make money but also made her feel more comfortable, managing responsibilities and tasks satisfactorily. At the time, she knew very well that these activities took time from her work on the thesis. Molly would have liked to work with another student on the thesis, and this was an option in her study programme. However, their professor recommended that all students wrote their thesis alone, to increase their chances of writing a PhD, promoting an understanding of individual, independent writing as a primary standard of 'academic potential' (Burke & Crozier, 2014), rather than, for instance, collaborative (writing) abilities. After this, everybody wanted to write their thesis alone, and Molly felt lost. Writing alone was a big challenge for her, and she fell behind. After a period of doing fieldwork abroad, she moved in with two other students, who were also writing their theses. They suggested that they all sit together and write, as mutual support, but Molly avoided this:

> *We could have . . . sat together and done the writing and my friend did offer to do that actually. But honestly, I think it just started preying on my mind even more living with those two, who were doing what I couldn't do, what I couldn't seem to accomplish.*

Rather than seizing the opportunity for support, the flatmates' offer triggered Molly's guilty conscience and low self-esteem. Molly was ashamed of her inability to perform the way she thought she should, not finding herself able to write on her own. Maybe similar feelings would have arisen for Molly had she in fact written her thesis with another student. However, the dismissal of co-writing as a legitimate way of organizing thesis work was related to a professor's elitist framing of all students as future PhD students, involving competitive social practices in the educational setting that determined the ambitions and work routines students were supposed to have. In the end, this was significant for Molly's experience of shame and her disinclination to make use of the offer to write together.

Molly's feeling of shame extended from the educational context to affect how she related to her friends and to getting support from them in general. Being ambivalent about the categorization of 'mentally ill,' she tried to keep her anxiety as well as her sense of inferiority a secret, and she withdrew from social life:

> *There, in a way, I felt that I was walking around with a secret . . . or something I had to navigate my social life around, I suppose mostly to avoid social events. But when I did interact, I tried to sort of, I didn't feel like I had a lot to contribute, but I tried to be the sort of person who listens and then just listen to what the others* [laughs] *were talking about, if we were in a group.*

Molly's more general sense of not having "much to offer" shows how a student's reaction to a single, maybe rash, comment from a professor can sometimes grow into a global sense of personal deficit. We should not dismiss such events as one student's (over)reaction to an unfortunate remark, even if this process primarily takes place in a private or individual domain. To Molly, her experience of difficulty in writing alone also affected her identity as a student. Over time, Molly turned against herself as an unworthy student:

> *For example right now, when things are going okay . . . then I might get a kind of idea that . . . that I'm too slow or that what I'm doing might not be useful after all, and then it just amounts to some nervousness that I'm doing it wrong or something.*

What we notice here is that even at a point in time where Molly feels she is doing 'okay' she worries and blames herself for being 'too slow' or doing her fieldwork and other parts of her thesis in the 'wrong' way. She has become ashamed of her performance, nervous and insecure about the demands to pass the final exams, even insecure about her judgemental abilities, and ultimately doubts if she 'is right' for the study programme (Colley et al., 2003).

Being in a 'weak role': dilemmas of getting (formal) support

The focus on individual performance, on working and writing independently, seems to be a recurrent theme in many of the students' stories regarding valuation, self-valuation and the experience of oneself as a suitable or worthy student of the particular programme. The image of the independent and hardworking student takes on a certain significance, when students with psychosocial problems need formal support, as we shall see in this section.

Signe is a 26-year-old student of physiotherapy, diagnosed with bipolar disorder. Signe, unlike Molly, describes herself as very open about her diagnosis and needs, and her experience of being open is generally good, although she has also faced the dilemma that people's preconceptions of people with mental illness are often loaded with stereotypes:

> *I don't feel like a stereotypical mentally ill nutter, . . . Rather, I think I have my own approach to it, my own openness around it, so I am not like: "Oh yeah, I'm just so stupid and weak and all that stuff." That changes, though, when I'm feeling bad, then an entirely different side of me comes out. But then again, as I am feeling now, I'm quite calm about knowing – for the most part – what I can do, that I'm not some lunatic running around and unable to achieve anything academically either. So right now I feel calm about it, you know? And because I'm at peace with it myself, I think many people reflect that back.*

Before entering higher education, Signe contacted the student counsellor to discuss her need to study part time. In Signe's experience, to have some flexibility in responding to her highs and lows was important to be able to keep up with her studies. She was told, however, that in practice part time is not an option in her study programme where strict progression and practice placements set the agenda. Therefore, Signe had to find other ways to adapt.

She feels it was important to be in a good class:

> *You get to know their strengths and then you can, like, talk to them, discuss with them. Some students know me . . ., oh, that bipolar girl . . . so sometimes I can have really bad days, and just the fact that only some people know, I think . . . that's a nice feeling, not to have to feel like I'm starting from scratch. But there are only some people that know. Then I don't need to explain anything, and I feel safe when I'm with those people, you see?*

Being open about good and bad days and being met with understanding in a 'good class' enabled Signe to come to school even on bad days, and also to get help from other students, when sometimes she couldn't be present. The diagnostic notion of bipolarity provided Signe with a vocabulary and a platform for developing an understanding of herself, everyday strategies and access to certain forms of support, not only from her classmates, but also more formal support like access to a psychiatrist, a psychiatric nurse and the student counsellor. They all gave Signe a "professional validation" that she was "not just lazy, and not just stupid, and I wasn't just nothing – instead there was a hormone in my brain that wasn't functioning as it should." They also acknowledged that studying is particularly hard for students with 'extra baggage.'

Nonetheless, Signe too had worries as to how others might interpret her and her 'extra baggage,' and what it might mean if categories from the psychiatric, diagnostic system entered the educational context:

> *It's not something I should misuse, but on the other hand, it can be quite nice sometimes to play that card, because then there's not so much to discuss, and it's not just me being weird, or bad in any sense, I have something, you know, physical, which makes certain things challenging for me. And it's as though because I have that, then I can be taken seriously and I am listened to . . .*

There was a fine line between when 'playing the card' seemed legitimate and when it was 'misuse.' This is a general concern for students related to receiving support. Support is somehow associated with the failure of being unable to complete your studies on your own or completing them by 'cheating.' To Signe, "it's not that there's anything wrong with asking for help." However, she and reportedly her fellow students all tended to think: 'This will pass – that is, it might just be me being a bit of a whiner, and everyone else also thinks this assignment is difficult,' making students 'disregard it' for too long before seeking help. Other students, however, told us about explicitly stigmatizing comments, pointing to, for example, extra time, assistance or aids as cheating. Signe usually came across as a competent, ambitious student. Asking for help was a dilemma, because she worried that it would undermine how those around her took her seriously as an academic student. Asking for help challenged her position as a competent and ambitious student, since 'competent' and 'needing help' come across as incompatible. She said:

> *When I am feeling well, like during my last placement here, I told my supervisor about it and she was like: "I would never have guessed." Because she's seen me function. But during my previous practice when I felt really bad, my supervisor was just . . . well, I could sense after I got better again later, that she had set the bar very low for me, she didn't really have high expectations of me.*

Here, the stigma and low expectations related to mental illness disturb the relationship between supervisor and student. Since the supervisor's expectations of her were 'too low,' it put Signe in a 'weak role,' made her work practice 'a bit boring' and 'didn't help her progress at all.' This made her worry about her learning curve while in education and, furthermore, about her future as a professional if she were to be seen as someone who cannot keep up or 'adjust to the workplace.'

In the higher education context, Signe distinguished between the category of 'mentally ill,' which held some kind of legitimacy, and more problematic categories of 'lazy,' 'stupid' or 'weak' students as opposed to ambitious, competent and strong students, better 'equipped' to deal with problems. This way of defining 'people with mental health problems' and 'normal people/students' as separate categories makes it difficult for students to formulate and orientate identity positions of simultaneously experiencing ill-being and being a competent student. Is it possible to maintain an identity as a good or normal student in higher education if you need help and support? If you in fact receive help and support, how is it possible to recognize and measure your performance in comparison with others? Dilemmas like these stem from dichotomous categories and neoliberal policy and carry experiences of shame and of being unworthy. One specific way in which this affects students is that they often refrain from disclosure and from seeking help and support (Storrie et al., 2010). Many students in our project, like Molly above, report that they hid or dismissed problems for a long time before acknowledging them or disclosing them to others.

As in Molly's case, Signe's dilemma of disclosing problems and still positioning herself as attractive extended beyond the academic or professional context. She seemed understood amongst students as clever and ambitious and a good student, but in private life and her free time, Signe would still feel alone. It was a dilemma to her, that on the one hand she needed to 'prioritize things that calm me down and give me energy' and she 'just loves' spending time going to classical music concerts or art museums by herself, taking this as 'breathing spaces' of an almost 'meditative' character. On the other hand, these priorities and settings do not match well with mainstream youth culture, for instance dating practices. Is it possible to find or be attractive to a boyfriend, if you are positioned in a 'weak role' in your study programme and if you don't like going to parties or dance halls? While she has few problems in being included in her study groups, Signe says:

> *It's more like personal relations that have seen it (bipolar disorder) as a huge problem, that I've had difficult periods, so . . . romantic relations, you could say, they haven't been able to accommodate me, it's been too much for them.*

This made Signe 'worry a lot' for the future, if and how she would ever get a partner and the children she hoped for. We see how dilemmas of how to work, how to lead your everyday life, how to present yourself and what to disclose affect students as they work through social practices and interactions amongst other students. We see how identity positions simultaneously relate to experiences of ill-being, of receiving support of different formal and informal kinds, of being a competent student and of being a young woman with dreams for her personal and romantic life. This thus extends from questions of work routines in educational settings to questions of 'belonging in this society' at large, as Alicia puts it in the introductory quote.

Be(com)ing 'right' for the programme: the project of self-correction

The analyses mentioned earlier show how the experiences of shame of Alicia, Molly and Signe relate to the valuation of them(selves) as wrong, inferior or weak in relation to study programmes with rather different study cultures. We have seen how valuation processes related to these study cultures interact with, and reinforce and are reinforced by, other dynamics in their lives: relations to other students and flatmates, romantic relations, public discourse and 'this society' at large. Thus, complex dynamics of higher education, youth culture and social differentiation are complicit in how Alicia, Molly and Signe feel 'right' or 'all wrong,' suitable or not, for their study programmes. Before closing this chapter, we return to Alicia to analyse her movement from 'feeling wrong' in Law School to reorienting herself and approaching higher education differently, becoming a 'proper' or more 'suitable' student in the School of Social Work (Burke & Crozier, 2014). The analysis shows how Alicia's learning and reflections from her first experience with higher education shape her way of entering and making herself at home, at ease and 'feeling right' in another study programme, at another point in time.

In retrospect, Alicia emphasizes how her sense of being the only one on the outside enhanced her feeling of shame and embarrassment to be unable to fulfil the expectations of students at Law School. The shame of not finishing what she had started kept Alicia hanging on to Law School for more than three years, while her family became increasingly worried and eventually urged her to leave. Not until a doctor more or less by chance identified a substantial weight loss did Alicia get help. She joined a therapy programme for youth with eating disorders.

Admittedly, the programme also helped Alicia to overcome some of her issues with eating, but what she describes in the interviews as the most important achievement of the programme is that it led to her discovery of other students with problems. This became an important turning point for her. She says:

> *There I was with other girls, and they were all really nice, and very bright and well-spoken and so on and they'd all dropped out of a study programme and started over again two times* **at a minimum**, *and I hadn't at that time. . . . And I remember thinking – "if they can do that, and if they're so cool, and if I think they're so great anyway, well it doesn't mean anything for what I think of them . . . then I can too. To hell with it, I'll leave".*

In the therapy group, Alicia could observe other students and their chains of argument regarding higher education. The therapy group was a safe space to discuss issues and worries related to higher education to realize that these were experiences shared by other students, and that leaving a study programme *and* being 'cool' could be an option. Eventually, Alicia left Law School after being formally enrolled for 4.5 years, 1.5 of these on sick leave.

When Alicia re-entered higher education, many things had changed. Years had passed and Alicia was in a better place 'personally.' She had spent two or three years in therapy, while also completing private education as a legal secretary. During this time, she also moved in with a childhood friend as her flatmate. She describes how she had 'become more forgiving towards myself, where I used to be very restrictive.' She says:

> *I've become another person along the way, and when you've taken many knocks . . . you have to constantly try to think of solutions – now what do I do, if I did that could I feel better or . . . So I think that it has, this can develop if you get help to get through it, then it can make you grow a lot because you've dealt with some emotions, and some things that you wouldn't have done otherwise.*

Furthermore, Alicia notes herself that 'time has changed' the educational policy climate, and that this might have influenced the fact that evaluation processes and listening to students' thoughts on study activities seemed to her to be more important in her new programme than in the previous one. She comments that at the School of Social Work "they've made a point of saying that you should make use of each other, that you should be able to feel good at your school, and let each other know."

Alicia describes how the way she started studying was also different. For instance, before arriving at the School of Social Work on the first day, she studied the list of students, and during introduction days, she made an enormous effort to establish social relationships with other students. This was how she met Cecilie, who came to be of huge significance for Alicia, providing the social relationship and sense of belonging she never found at Law School. Throughout the first term, Alicia found it hard to attend classes if she was not feeling well, but Cecilie suggested that they could meet outside the school building and enter together, or even at the train station to go together on the bus, and frequently texted Alicia to check up on her. Alicia was excited that someone was 'looking out for me.' On most days, this got her to school even if she was not feeling too well. If she did not turn up, Cecilie would hand over information on what was said and what went on. When Cecilie felt down, Alicia did the same things for her. Together, Alicia reports, she and Cecilie tried to encourage a generally inclusive and open environment, such as by taking into their group a student who was excluded from his initial study group. In different ways, they would work to establish an open and professional way of discussing their expectations for each other and for the work processes in the study groups. The social belonging and the academic learning merged: The sense of 'basically feeling secure' in the learning environment, the fact that somebody would notice 'if I turn up or not' and 'keep a seat for you,' and that you had 'someone to go for coffee with during break,' helped Alicia to get to class even on bad days.

As in Law School, artefacts as concrete symbols of community membership and as drivers in social routines during breaks, in lecture halls, etc. seemed to play an important role. At the School of Social Work, the crux seemed to be coffee:

> *There's a massive coffee culture among students (laughs), it's almost like you're an outsider if you don't drink a latte (laughs), so it means a lot to be able to go down with the others to the cafeteria, buy an apple or eat lunch or buy a cup of coffee, because there's sort of a culture around that, it's a community thing . . .*

Money still mattered as a means to access artefacts involved in one's activity, but amounts needed were significantly smaller, such as 'seven kroner for a cup of coffee,' rather than thousands of kroner for a Gucci bag. Being part of the social community was of direct importance in accessing the academic content as well. Going for coffee, you 'can ask, oh, did you get that text, did you understand what he said at the end?' If you missed class one day, you had somebody to fill you in. With other students, there was a forum for processing course material. As Alicia says: "When I'm in the study group and you're discussing some of the subject matter, what you get out of that, it's incredible the difference it makes."

Alicia's sense of being a worthy student grew at the School of Social Work. She was more satisfied with her own work routines. For instance, she would read and prepare by herself at home or even on the train, which used to be a problem. She sensed that 'people think I'm all right, they think I'm good at writing, they want to be in my group.' Other students approached her with their doubts, looking for advice, because they believed she would listen. Positive feedback from teachers and supervisors also contributed to her academic confidence, even when her marks were poor:

> *It's very, very, very motivating when you're acknowledged for a good performance. . . . But I was also told, at an exam where we messed up the learning goals, where we studied the wrong things, in our first year. . . . Well, I was told, even though I got a D, she said, "How all of you could have misunderstood the assignment, in a group of five people, I really don't know." But she told me,*

"Well, you have difficulties with this and that, but I can tell that you have a good appreciation of this field, you have an eye for what might be relevant to look into." And even though I got a D, I felt like I could float out of the door because of the positive feedback I got – not just "Hey, this was really stupid," but that she actually acknowledged me like "I can tell you've reflected properly on this, you really understand what this means," so . . . a compliment (laughs).

Alicia compares this pedagogical approach to that of Law School and points out that at Social Work it was "*much easier to approach a teacher and say, 'I'm a bit uncertain about this and that.'*" She explains that this is due to a more informal and familiar culture between teachers and students, where 'we know each other' and Alicia felt that 'this is actually my school.' She particularly emphasizes how teachers worked to facilitate and 'establish an atmosphere' where students 'dare to try something out.' She says:

We had one teacher that I almost fell in love with (laughs), because he had this great energy, and he was so good at creating a feeling of community with his words, I mean, just the way he spoke, like he acknowledged us, you see? He always said, "Go out and discuss with your colleagues", that means the other students. No one else calls us colleagues, like if we already . . . he was like "You know so many things, we're actually already sort of colleagues," like this acknowledgement . . . They're good at making fun of things, saying what they think themselves about something, and you get a sense of what kind of person this is . . .

Another aspect that Alicia appreciated was how the academic curriculum provided a new framework for understanding herself and her process. She says:

The course material is incredibly interesting, and in fact, you learn a lot about yourself and get very aware of yourself in social situations and conflicts. You have to be aware and . . . um, reflect on your own practice, how you position yourself with clients, power relations and all that. Suddenly, you realize this in your own private relationships. Actually, I like that. You notice it. And maybe you can change it.

Specifically, Alicia elaborates on her reading of Hartmut Rosa's analyses of acceleration as a 'revelation' and says, "I'd marry him on the spot." To her, Rosa's analyses and concepts were very meaningful, "the truest of truths" and described her experiences in ways that "I haven't been good enough at expressing or defining myself." Working with this theoretical framework shifted her perspective on her own history and situation and in some ways even changed her everyday practice. She particularly describes a collective 'hypocrisy' regarding understandings and images of 'good students':

All this pressures you to perform more, quicker, finer, better – that mill just never stops turning. You have to optimize yourself, and if you don't, you can just lay down and die. . . . Hell, we can't keep up. You build some narrative around the good student being able to do this, and then 99.9% of all students can go around feeling inadequate compared to this mannequin of how you should be as a student which no one is able to live up to. . . . You can't point to a single person you know who's like that . . . I think that's uncanny . . .

The 'narrative of the good student' and the collective 'hypocrisy' in higher education

The experiences of shame of Alicia, Molly and Signe are examples of how students negotiate and value themselves and each other in relation to institutionalized notions of the good and proper student (Burke & Crozier, 2014). Inspired by concepts of 'proper,' 'suitable' or 'valued' students, we have attempted to turn a critical eye to the narratives and moral structures at work in the educational settings we have explored when following Alicia, Molly and Signe. How are they complicit in students' shame and self-sorting processes?

The aforementioned analysis shows how students like Alicia, Molly and Signe are challenged as participants and as legitimate students in higher education. An overriding higher education focus on students' independent, individual performance is complicit in their experience of shame, involving feelings of being wrong, not having much to offer or being in a weak role. Also complicit are differentiated profiles of study programmes and the particular student profiles programmes present as 'suitable' for them.

There are no simple explanations of who or what (de)values Molly, Signe and Alicia, or which parameters guide (e)valuations of students' suitability or worth. For instance, Alicia's experiences from Law School, for better or worse, inform her ways of experiencing and navigating in the Social Work programme. They also inform her understanding and (re)construction of herself, through her framing of failures and successes, as a worthy, suitable student and future social work practitioner (Colley et al., 2003). We should acknowledge the empowering and positive storyline as well as the critical reflexive levels in Alicia's story. We should also consider critical perspectives on the societal dynamics and selection processes behind Alicia's discovery of the study programme, which is 'right for me.' What might on a personal level be an empowering experience could simultaneously be interpreted as sorting processes on a structural level, pushing particular students out of law into social work.

The explorations of students' experiences of shame have led us on to different dimensions and ideas of 'good students,' thought to be robust and healthy, easily accustomed to higher education, working and performing individually and independently, completing their education and finding a job as the way to societal recognition. Equally institutionalized notions of young people with 'mental difficulties' are that they are (chronically) vulnerable or ill, academically 'weak,' require support and extra resources, and are at high risk of not completing their education and not finding employment (on ordinary terms). Such dichotomous categorizations entail the risk that many students with psychosocial problems will be understood by fellow students, staff and themselves as people failing to live up to the 'narrative of the good student,' those who do not belong in higher education. This chapter has taken the first steps in showing how becoming processes, where students come to understand themselves as students who are not proper, suitable or good, and who do not belong in higher education, play out in the intersections of student biography, higher education institutions and study cultures, societal discourses and students' hopes and fears for the future. In the analyses in the following three chapters, we will develop in further detail how students with psychosocial problems battle with work routines related to particular temporal structures, with feeling safe in the learning community and with the dilemmas and extra work of getting the support they need.

Molly's, Signe's and Alicia's identity processes related to higher education consist of developing ways to work, cope and get better; coming to terms with academic interests, learning ambitions and professional direction and contemplating on who they would like to be and in which contexts they thrive. The analysis shows the complexity and intersections of students' personal history and current situation, the facilitation of the learning environment by higher education institutions and their staff, student interactions and communities and broader, societal discourses on student characteristics and responsibilities. It shows how all of these factors are at work in students' identity processes, whether related to the curriculum, the work routines, the community, the formal support or the personal direction dimensions of higher education, through which they position and reposition themselves and come to understand and develop meta-perspectives on themselves as good or worthy members of academic and social communities.

Note

1 Alicia's mother works as a self-taught consultant, her father as an independent craftsman.

References

Brown, R. (2018). Subtile sorteringsprocesser i den linjedelte folkeskole. [Subtle sorting processes in programme divided schools]. *Dansk Pædagogisk Tidsskrift*, *2018*(2), 37–48.

Burke, P. J. (2017). Difference in higher education pedagogies: Gender, emotion and shame. *Gender and Education*, *29*(4), 430–444. https://doi.org/10.1080/09540253.2017.1308471

Burke, P. J., & Crozier, G. (2014). Higher education pedagogies: Gendered formations, mis/recognition and emotion. *Journal of Research in Gender Studies*, *4*(2), 52–67.

Colley, H., James, D., Diment, K., & Tedder, M. (2003). Learning as becoming in vocational education and training: Class, gender and the role of vocational habitus. *Journal of Vocational Education & Training*, *55*(4), 471–498. http://dx.doi.org/10.1080/13636820300200240

Frost, L. (2016). Exploring the concepts of recognition and shame for social work. *Journal of Social Work Practice*, *30*(4), 431–446. http:/dx.doi.org/10.1080/026 50533.2015.1132689

Jimenez, L., & Walkerdine, V. (2011). A psychosocial approach to shame, embarrassment and melancholia amongst unemployed young men and their fathers. *Gender and Education*, *23*(2), 185–199.

Larsen, L., Weber, S. S., & Wulf-Andersen, T. (2020). Asynkronitet og sortering i et accelereret uddannelsessystem [Asynchrony and sorting in an accelerated educational system]. *Dansk Pædagogisk Tidsskrift*, *1*, 35–49.

Loveday, V. (2016). Embodying deficiency through 'affective practice': Shame, relationality, and the lived experience of social class and gender in higher education. *Sociology*, *50*(6), 1140–1155.

Rosa, H. (2013). *Social acceleration: A new theory of modernity*. Columbia University Press.

Scheff, T. (2014). The ubiquity of hidden shame in modernity. *Cultural Sociology*, *8*(2), 129–141.

Skeggs, B. (1997). *Formation of class and gender: Becoming respectable*. Sage.

Skeggs, B. (2011). Imagining personhood differently: Person value and autonomist working-class value practices. *The Sociological Review*, *59*(3), 496–513.

Soldatic, K., & Morgan, H. (2017). "The way you make me feel": Shame and the neoliberal governance of disability welfare subjectivities in Australia and the UK. In J. Louth & M. Potter (Eds.), *Edges of identity: The production of neoliberal subjectivities* (pp. 106–133). University of Chester Press.

Storrie, K., Ahern, K., & Tuckett, A. (2010). A systematic review: Students with mental health problems – a growing problem. *International Journal of Nursing Practice*, *16*, 1–6.

Thomsen, J. P. (2021). The social class gap in bachelor's and master's completion: University dropout in times of educational expansion. *Higher Education*. https://doi.org/10.1007/s10734-021-00726-3

6 "I cannot even set the pace." Asynchronicity and inequality in an accelerated educational system

> *The very second I finish my studies I will just travel away to a place where I myself decide the pace and I myself decide what I want to plan for the day, where I can always say, that's enough now. Because sometimes it feels like you're caught in one of those hamster wheels. I have to get up, I have to go to work, and today I have to study and I have to read this and that. I really feel like I'm in a hamster wheel because there is always something I must do and I cannot even set the pace.*

Jannie, a 23-year-old female student, thus seems to compare her life with a hamster wheel in which she is out of control in managing her own time. She dreams about 'pulling the plug' and getting a break from all the different time structures she is battling with. Jannie is in her third semester of a bachelor's programme in the humanities. She has no diagnoses but struggles with time pressure and a lack of belonging in higher education. The feeling of running in a hamster wheel makes it difficult for her to belong in higher education, and she blames herself for not being able to time manage her life. She has moved several times and is still having difficulty finding a suitable place to live, which takes time and also puts her under pressure.

This chapter shows the subjective dimensions of how temporal structures in higher education contribute to student inequality and lead to continuous battles against time. We analyse how temporal demands seem to be paramount in students' negotiations of legitimacy and belonging in higher education and society, and this applies particularly to students with psychosocial problems. Until now, the focus on inequality in Denmark has typically been related to political agendas about social mobility and breaking the so-called negative social legacy. The question of inequality is primarily discussed from the perspective of students from non-academic backgrounds. Classical sociology of education has in different ways pointed out how the educational system functions as 'sorting machines' (Bernstein, 2001; Bourdieu, 1996; Domina et al., 2017). For many different reasons, students with psychosocial problems may have difficulty in following the dominant time structures in higher education, which for some of them become a separate issue contributing to inequality.

The chapter draws on empirical work from/with three female students, Jannie, Esther and Nanna, for whom fighting against time is highly important in their

DOI: 10.4324/9781003221029-6

battles for recognition and belonging in higher education. The three students are involved in three different kinds of battles with time: Jannie to be recognized as capable of managing the time structure of her everyday life, especially balancing study time and paid work and other activities she wants to and has to participate in. Nanna struggles with the consequences of falling behind both academically and socially, while Esther is battling with taking too long over her education and especially the related embarrassment of not following the dominant time structures. We present the three of them throughout the chapter in relation to selected relevant themes: being out of control of time, the time structure and pace of European Credit Transfer System (ECTS) credits, to be an asynchronous student, and time as social differentiation and a signifier of belonging.

Theoretically, the chapter is informed by Rosa's sociology of time (2013), which emphasizes the general acceleration of society. Rosa points out that the struggle for recognition is (also) a battle for and against time. The chapter also draws on Bennett and Burke's (2017) work on re/conceptualizing time and temporality in higher education, where they emphasize that time, that is, having enough time and time pressure, has become one of the most stressful aspects of learning. Dominant discourses about time and time limits determine who is constructed or recognized as capable in higher education (Bennett & Burke, 2017). Further, time relates to pedagogical codes and the importance of being able to speak the expected legitimate pedagogical text, as Bernstein's educational sociology (2001) would have it. Bernstein himself is not especially interested in time as such but does analyse how a curriculum is structured, for example, by rules of order and tempo, which students have to decode and live up to (Bernstein, 2001).

In this chapter, we thus draw on these scholars to ask how time and the highlighting of tempo (above learning) are experienced by students, how this relates to students' psychosocial problems and how particular notions of time affect students' understandings of who belongs in higher education. We argue that the focus on speed and on managing and optimizing time contribute to the sorting of students by ignoring the fact that their diverse life circumstances give them varying amounts of time to study, while students with psychosocial problems can be unequally challenged by time in different ways (cf. Chapter 5).

Out of control: student life as a jigsaw of time

As Rosa (2013) points out, an acceleration of time has taken place in late capitalist societies and movement has been an objective in itself. An important feature of contemporary society is not having time, being busy, and being constantly in a hurry. To stand still is to lag behind, and whoever lags behind has only himself or herself to blame (Rosa, 2013). As mentioned initially, Jannie feels a great deal of pressure to be able to find time for everything. She says:

> *I also try to see my friends occasionally. I've started cutting down on it because I haven't got the time and because I cannot afford it, because I've had a lot of stress with my money. And that has been – at least the last few months – the*

> *biggest pressure on my studies. There's been a lot at least in relation to my studies where I have seen I did not have time to read because I had to work. And then I also have a boyfriend I have to find time for. So he has to fit into all of this too. And it's really a jigsaw puzzle, you have to move the pieces around and see where they fit and so on.*

Using the jigsaw metaphor, Jannie here illustrates how she battles to manage the different timescapes (Adam, 2008; Bennett & Burke, 2017) of her everyday life and how she feels that she has insufficient time. The concept of timescapes captures the complexity and the many aspects of time and points out that it is still traditional trajectories that are recognized as 'the right way' to study (Bennett & Burke, 2017, p. 2). Jannie follows the recommended timeline for her programme but several students fall behind because they are under time pressure. The acceleration of life tempo, as Rosa defines it, in combination with the dominant labour market of higher education makes it necessary for students to start their career long before they graduate. For that reason, many students have paid work several hours per week to strengthen their employability. As described in Chapter 2, although students in Denmark receive financial support, the cost of living is very high. Especially, housing costs are shooting up, necessitating paid work besides studying. For Jannie too, the jigsaw of time primarily requires her to do considerable paid work to pay her rent, but as the above quotation shows, she has trouble fulfilling all the different demands because of insufficient time. This leads to a feeling of being out of control and Jannie therefore wonders whether she should take a break after finishing her bachelor's degree. Further, this is also a question of 'important aspects of the broader experience of being a higher education student' (Brooks et al., 2021, p. 8), and for Jannie the time pressure becomes a question of whether and how she feels capable as a university student.

Esther is a 31-year-old female student who has recently graduated from a master's programme in social science. For years, she has suffered from depressions and obsessive-compulsive disorder and has been examined for other diagnoses. She feels that depressions bother her most and the complexity of her psychosocial problems make life difficult for her. Esther has two sisters, whom she describes as 'very academic,' which implies that they are more academic than her. Her parents have suggested that she drop out, wanting to protect their daughter from all the trouble studying entails for her but she is very determined to complete. She is very frustrated that she is not able to study as much and as fast as she wants to and feels she has to:

> *I have not been proud of it. And because I, well, I just think I should have finished 100 years ago. So that has overshadowed my studies. And I have not, well, it has not crossed my mind at all, that is, the idea of celebrating it in any way.*

Rather than being proud of graduating, Esther seems embarrassed that her psychosocial problems and mental illness have made her spend too many extra years to complete her master's degree. Of course, she is happy to finally have completed her education. Her family is relieved because it has been a very hard time for her and for them. However, she is not proud at all. Mostly, she is ashamed that she spent almost twice as long as other students, almost ten years, to complete her education. This shows how time structures are linked to recognition structures: to be recognized as a graduate and an academic you have to complete in normal time.

During her studies, time was important to Esther in different ways: she wanted her life to be more structured, she spent considerable time on different kinds of treatments "and then a lot of attempts at studying" and her periods of illness made her fall behind. Esther is blaming herself that she is "ridiculously bad at keeping a good structure each day." Further, she explains it in this way:

> *I have a hard time getting up, but I also have an equally hard time going to bed. It's because, in the evening I often start feeling ashamed that I haven't done everything I could, and then I think I should try to make up for it. And then I try to do something, kind of halfway, but in fact I'm a bit too tired and so on. So sometimes these evenings can be kind of . . . then it can all fall apart. And because I find it hard to accept that I can't just make up for it. Then it often ends up that I just collapse into my bed with my clothes on.*

Esther seems to have entered a vicious circle: doing too little, and then blaming herself (cf. Chapter 5), which produces an even worse time structure. Time structuring is a major issue to her and such battles against time structure and herself are an ongoing process for her. She withdraws from friends and different kinds of social life. Asked about her typical week (cf. Chapter 3), she answers:

> *I'm pretty sure that if you'd been following me with a little camera all autumn, I don't think you could say I had a basic template for a week. I don't think I've had that for a very long time, but I still aim to have one. So I try, I'm always dreaming of getting one.*

Like Jannie, Esther feels out of control in managing time in her life but in a different way. She is convinced that if she has a better time structure for each day and week, she will feel better and be more productive, and then be a better student. Esther also associates time with tempo, that is, how much activity is possible in a given timeframe, which makes her feel very misrecognized by herself, by higher education and by society. With reference to Rosa, time has become a competition parameter required by different societal institutions (Rosa, 2013). The subjective experience of this is the feeling of time pressure. The time structure in higher education tells students to allocate 43 hours per week to study activities defined by a narrow time schedule dictating when to do what. This scheduled time structure ignores the fact that students have other needs and obligations to friends, doctor's appointments, the search for housing, paid work, etc. This situation causes inequality; parental support becomes necessary and spending much time on finding a place to live influences the way students belong or not in higher education and their attitudes to learning.

ECTS time: pace before content

As argued earlier, societal acceleration makes tempo one of the most important timescapes (Adam, 2008). As part of society, higher education has also become accelerated and here tempo has become important in different ways, such as 'ECTS time' as Bengtsen et al. (2021) define the time structure in higher education. In the Danish context, Sarauw and Madsen (2020) argue that the orientation towards progress and economic motives places higher education today in the 'paradigm of speed.' The Bologna Process frames and structures time in higher education in a very powerful way and local and national politics can further reinforce this (Sarauw & Madsen, 2016, 2020). As described in Chapter 2, the ECTS in general is constructed around time, defined as "the time students typically need to complete all learning activities (such as lectures, seminars, projects, practical work, self-study and examinations) required to achieve the expected learning outcomes" (EU, 2015, p. 36). In Denmark, recent educational reforms have introduced (non-transparent) requirements for progress, fast tracking and performance in completing higher education, which emphasizes the focus on the intensity (i.e. the time spent studying each week) and the recommended courses of study. Standards for how much time students have to spend completing their study programmes have been determined; all students must be full-time students, thus spending 43 hours a week on their studies as mentioned earlier. A linear understanding of progression also accelerates the curriculum. The intention of the module structure is flexibility in order and place but the result (at least in Denmark) is that learning has become instrumental and students' attitudes and strategies have also become more instrumental.

Students naturally try to decode and fulfil the demands and expectations they encounter in higher education, including the notions of time. Jannie naturally also does this and as mentioned earlier she follows the recommended timeline. She calls herself very 'sociable.' Social relations are very important to her and closely linked to her motivation to study. In the beginning of her university career, she lives with two other girls, with whom she also works in her class activities. After a while, one of them distances herself from Jannie and she begins to feel much pressure both personally and academically. She has a particular battle to find enough time to study as much as she thinks she is supposed to and as much as she wants to. This makes her see duty in opposition to desire. She says:

> *I just think I want to have more time and energy to get it done. And for me, it's also the thing that maybe I actually have the time, but I just haven't got the desire to do it. Because sometimes I might even choose to say: "Okay, maybe I should just relax now, because I've been busy" instead of maybe getting it done instead.*

Jannie experiences ECTS time (Bengtsen et al., 2021) as a feeling that time and desire are intertwining in a way that makes her unsure if the university is the right place for her. This shows how the general time pressure in higher education becomes individualized and it becomes a question of students' motivation to study. Furthermore, for Jannie it is a question of her ability to manage her time:

> *so I haven't, I cannot find the time to read the things I have to. And I think it's difficult to make priorities, because I want to achieve it all, but everyone also tells me that you have to prioritize your things.*

Obviously, Jannie has learned that time management is about prioritizing, and two things challenge her. She wants to be well prepared by reading everything the students are asked to read and thus not prioritize, and if she has to prioritize then how to do it? In her effort to achieve this, she is on her own and apparently no teachers are helping her. One of her classmates sometimes helps her: "But I don't talk so much to people about what it is, the programme and the homework and so on, I think."

The timescape in higher education places tempo before learning and an important skill today is to master time management. Here Bennett and Burke (2017, p. 5) argue that challenges students might face may not simply be understood as a question of being better at managing time. This notion both individualizes social relations to time and ignores structural disadvantages and inequalities and other ways of relating to time.

Nanna is also battling against time but in a different way from Jannie and Esther. Nanna is 30 years old and is in her second semester of a master's programme in health care. She has suffered from stress, anxiety and depression but has almost recovered. From the very beginning, she decides not to take any medications but to recover on her own and with help from a psychotherapist. She falls behind because of illness and battles with how to emphasize learning more than marks. Nanna puts it this way:

> *When I went back and took 5 or 10 ECTS after I had been ill and managed it all by writing by myself – that was great and then I learnt that marks don't represent who I am as a person. I still focus on marks, but I try to avoid it. I focus on learning rather than marks . . .*

According to Rosa (2013), time management has become a very important skill in following the societal tempo and its time structures. With Bernstein's concepts, students try to live up to both the regulatory discourse (rules of social order/hierarchical rules) and the teaching discourse (rules of selection, order, tempo and criteria) (Bernstein, 2001). In particular, time and tempo have become significant in terms of both completing programmes fast and following the tempo in the curriculum. Some of the rules are very visible (visible pedagogy), such as the numbers of ECTS per year, while others are more invisible (invisible pedagogy), such as how to prioritize the amount of literature to read.

102 *"I cannot even set the pace."*

Jannie also tries to decode and fulfil the expectations for pace and tempo, which has cost her a great deal of mental and emotional work. Here, her psychotherapist has also been helpful:

> *If I lower my expectations then I do better. So if I lower my expectations, I relax more. If I expect to read both Honneth and Adorno in one day, but instead spend two days on it. It's OK to not always do your very best. It is also OK if you do not do extremely well. The most important thing is to learn a lot. The devil in me sometimes says that the good student is the one who gets A all the time.*

Obviously, Jannie, like many other students in our data, reflects herself in a kind of ideal student studying theory at a high speed and getting good marks. Her psychotherapist tries to help her to control her 'inner devil' and Jannie has developed new strategies for studying and learning. Acceleration translates into the norms of what and how much one must achieve to be a good proper student (Burke & Crozier, 2014). Bernstein's educational sociology points out how overall forms of power and control outside the education system establish themselves as pedagogical communication within the system through the way in which individual programmes are classified and framed. The framework works in the form of rules for recognition and realization and rules for 1) social order (regulatory discourse) and 2) discursive order (teaching discourse) (Bernstein, 2001). These concepts help us to understand how students try to decode/identify and live up to the demands and expectations they are met with in their education. Burke et al. (2016) use the term 'capability' about the construction of how to be a proper student. An important social order is to do everything on time, and the teaching discourse requires students to follow the recommended study timeline. Students who are not 'on time' or do not master time management as expected are considered unsuitable to study or more or less (hopelessly) disorganized (Bennett & Burke, 2017). This illustrates the power of the time structure and time discourse in contemporary higher education; the legitimate pedagogical text is often and very directly linked to time through Bernstein's conceptualization of meeting deadlines and following the recommended courses of study as powerful time structures (Bernstein, 2001). Bernstein also points out that such rules and structures that demand being on time all the time cause inequality, since some students have more time for studying than others, depending on how much support they can get from their parents and how much paid work they need to have.

Right time is on time: asynchronous students

According to Adam (2008), another important timescape is timing, which means synchronization, coordination and right/wrong time. Part of the Danish Progress Reform (cf. Chapter 2) is that students who do not maintain the expected progress, and do not gain the required number of ECTS credits per semester, are immediately defined as asynchronous and call attention to themselves as problematic due to their 'delay' in time. According to the Danish Universities Act, undue delay is ultimately associated with the threat of termination. Asynchrony is not a new phenomenon in the Danish education system. Until the mid-1990s, for better or worse, not much attention was paid to students who exceeded the standard time limits. Not until students approached the category of 'eternal student' would they attract attention. Today, even minor delays are identified as a problem, as newer discourses about time have developed and higher education has installed different 'time pushers' to accelerate student completion, and the higher education timescape is now, as mentioned earlier, characterized by speed, progress and fast completion. In the educational system, we see the accelerated rhythms carried by incentives to make students enter higher education quickly, to move quickly through to completion and to quickly proceed from higher education to employment.

In our empirical work, we see some of the consequences of fast completion requirements and how these relate to recognition. One consequence is what happens when students fall behind. Some students feel pressured to return to their studies from sick leave before they have recovered completely. Nanna is one of them. She says:

> *I had sick leave and at first I was just trying to tell myself that I'm not writing a project... I wasn't going to. I went to the classes I could, but didn't get anything out of it, but I **had to** have the 5 ECTS – I went to our group meetings, but the others helped me get through.... I didn't get anything out of it.*

During the first months of her master's programme, she develops stress and anxiety and therefore tries to study on a part-time basis by postponing a project until the coming semester. The activity she participated in is organized as group work with the other members helping her, but as she says she did not learn anything. She needed a break, but instead she had a relapse. The demands for progress and ECTS credits make life difficult for students who become ill and have to take a break from their studies. Instead, they may have to follow one course despite being ill, and then it takes longer to get well again. Due to the implementation requirement, she still feels compelled to attend some of the classes, but without getting anything out of them or out of the work as a whole. Rosa (2013, p. 134) calls this: "The compulsion to adapt." This also demonstrates the ECTS time structure and how the different modules and other study activities are cut up into smaller bits defined by the number of ECTS credits. To Nanna, this becomes a question of getting credits on time rather than learning, and apparently, she was not given any information about what else to do. Time here is both a trigger and a particular space of subjectivity where she is fighting to come back on track. Time and ECTS have become more important than learning and Nanna's lived time does not correspond with the functional and linear ECTS time (Bengtsen et al., 2021). Subsequently, in the interview situation, Nanna also reasons as follows:

> *And then I could just feel after that exam that this isn't working, but I should have just done nothing. I shouldn't have taken the subject at that time, I had*

> *difficulty sleeping in general, but I couldn't sleep at all if I was going to the university the next day. I talked to the doctor about not having to go back that semester.*

Nanna often seems to need a break as she now finds it even more difficult to study, and the result of returning to the programme too early is that she has to go on sick leave again. She takes advance of the flexibility, but it comes at a price at the individual and personal level. Now she is in danger of falling farther behind and feels a lot of pressure. The effort to live up to the administrative norms of acceleration has in this case a dysfunctional deceleration as its downside (cf. Rosa, 2013, p. 84). The example of Nanna shows that illness and the associated need for breaks are not recognized at an institutional level in higher education and she is placed in the problematic category of an 'asynchronous' student. The word itself is an indication that right time is on time and wrong time is delay (Adam, 2008). Several students take advantage of the built-in flexibility and postpone some ECTS credits without major problems; but for students with psychosocial challenges, this often becomes problematic as it requires considerable effort to join new social and study communities (cf. Chapter 7).

Esther has also felt the frustration of returning to the programme too early after sick leaves, and concludes:

> *where the symptoms have decreased, but where I've still been a little shaky. Where it wouldn't take much to have a relapse. So it's been some **really** stupid short-term solutions which are the reason, and that's why I've been in the programme for nine years, because there have just been so many of those gaps. . . . It could have been done much more effectively, I think . . . I actually think I would have finished faster if I'd got only one but a longer sick leave where I knew like I was protected now.*

Esther is convinced that if she had had the opportunity to recover once and for all she would have been able to complete faster. Again, she is not able to see and emphasize that she did actually complete despite her serious challenges and she obviously focuses on the time structure and the dominant demands and discourses about tempo and timing.

The demands for progress and the related administrative rules order students like Nanna and Esther to return to studying without having recovered sufficiently. Esther is an example of how such rules might have the opposite result to the one intended, and it was Esther who paid the price for battling between two dominant discourses of time: the 'eternal student' discourse and the discourse of time discipline. Both of them are embarrassing: the first one because it is associated with laziness and lack of focus and the second one because she fails to live up to it. This shows how time discipline is part of the hidden curriculum in school and higher education (Brooks et al., 2021). Nanna and especially Esther are unable to follow the intended study progression, which places them in vulnerable positions. Nanna succeeded in getting back on track on her own, whereas Esther became more and more frustrated and embarrassed at spending so many years completing her education. According to Rosa, acceleration on the subjective side can give an experience of standing on a "slide." A break from the set pace is not felt to be a break, but a relapse (Rosa, 2013, p. 157) where one has to do more and more to keep up if one wants to succeed (Rosa, 2013, p. 134, cf. also p. 173). Bengtsen et al. (2021) emphasize that the conditions for recognition are closely linked to if and how one keeps to one's time; here, time is understood as functional and linear and far from corresponding with 'lived time.' The analytical distinctions between time and timescape (Bennett & Burke, 2017) or functional time and lived time (Bengtsen et al., 2021) are helpful to understand how students are challenged in managing their everyday life.

Brooks et al. (2021) argue that changes in time not only relate to the European Bologna Process but also may be understood as far more complicated and fundamental changes in societal processes. Despite the general tendencies of Europeanization, timescapes differ considerably by nation, depending on how 'university time' is understood. Different traditions of higher education, the mechanisms through which degrees are funded and national policy are important factors (Brooks et al., 2021). Here, Denmark (as well as Germany) is distinct from other European countries by having 'flexible and loosely bounded student timescapes' (Brooks et al., 2021, p. 7), which means that students to a greater extent control their own time. This is currently under great pressure by reforms encouraging students to progress more quickly and complete faster. With the concept of timescapes, Bennett and Burke underline that time is not only clock and calendar; it is embedded in social and cultural dynamics of power and inequality (Bennett & Burke, 2017). In this sense, time does not exist without context – it is not neutral. Bennett and Burke emphasize how dominant notions of time define who is included or excluded, and capability to study relates to notions of time.

Asynchrony: time as social differentiation

Sick leaves or leaves in general reveal another aspect of social acceleration: namely, how social acceleration brings about constant changes in the institutions. When Nanna returns to her programme, there is (again) a new curriculum:

> *When I came back, it was really hard, a new curriculum had come, I was on the old one, and I was trying to figure out what that meant for me. It was **really** difficult to figure out what would happen. They haven't decided on the reading list. . . . There has been huge confusion – can I take the exam with the new curriculum with the others, or can't I?*

Returning to one's studies after leave of absence can be very difficult since many things might have changed. Higher education institutions are also accelerating with regular reforms, changes of curriculum, reorganization of administrative procedures, complicated regulations and complicated rules for waivers. The result of the constant changes becomes clear from the uncertainty of "what it means for me." The individual loses her "action-oriented experiences" (Rosa, 2013, p. 76). The result is perceived as lack of control, chaos and unpredictability, which is expressed in the students' experience of *"huge confusion."* This confusion reflects a great deal of bureaucratic hassle, uncertainty and frustration in educational institutions. To Nanna, it produces alienation and lack of resonance (Rosa, 2013), which do not lead to feelings of belonging.

Like Nanna, Esther also talks about the rapid changes in the curriculum:

so in terms of planning my studies and so on, I think I'm also using a lot of energy right now and I've written emails and that . . . to figure out what I can do with . . . they rang me before Christmas and they'd found out that I needed five more credits . . . well ok, but I have had several curricula, and I myself had lost track.

It is easy to lose track when one falls behind, and for Esther this meant that the university administration contacted her when she was writing her master's thesis to tell her that she needed five more ECTS credits. She got lost in the various curricula she had used, and the fact that she needed credits knocked her out and she was confused about what to do now. This is another example of how ECTS time structures time in higher education, while Ester's lived time (Bengtsen et al., 2021) is structured quite differently, mostly because of her periods of illness.

Becoming an asynchronous student also affects one's social life, both because such students are seen as students who cannot be on time and because they lose connections to social and study communities when they drop out of their classes. When Esther finally has to start writing her master's thesis, it is difficult for her to find another student as co-writer:

But obviously after a few years, both because of my leave, but also because of my illness, I'm about to. . . . In recent years, I haven't known a soul at the University. When I have been there to get some credits, it has been very sporadic. For example, when I went to a thesis start-up event before Christmas where you're supposed to find a partner, I could see wow! . . . Here I was obviously at a disadvantage, because people were sitting there almost arm in arm. Most of them wanted to write alone and the others came with the students they'd been with throughout the programme. So there I could easily feel that my timeline was not exactly straight down the road.

Esther feels lonely and excluded from the group of students who are going to write master's theses and she ends up with another female student, but their co-writing is very difficult as they had "no common frame of reference" as Esther expresses it. She feels she is paying a high price and sometimes she considers going solo – but she did not and finally they submitted their thesis and graduated.

Studying includes joining and participating in new and different groups and balancing life as a student with other activities and timescapes. Often, social and study communities are established at the beginning of a semester and then it can be difficult to keep up later, for example, after a period of illness or leave of absence. Therefore, one cannot easily find other students to identify and share experiences with if one has not been in contact with them from the start. With a more flimsy attachment to other students and their academic and social support, it is easier to feel lonely and excluded (cf. Chapter 7). Furthermore, students often describe themselves and their difficulty in participating based on more diffuse or implicit notions of what they should be able to do. When one cannot live up to fellow students', others' and one's own expectations of what it means to be a good proper student, this, as we will show, becomes a separate burden in student life.

Acceleration and desynchronization can also explain how the time perspective acquires a new and increased importance in the programmes, and how it contributes to a differentiation of the students into good (synchronized) and vulnerable (asynchronous) students.

Rosa understands desynchronization as a process in which "systemically institutionalized or structurally induced temporal patterns and perspectives, on the one hand, and the temporal patterns and perspectives of actors, on the other, increasingly diverge" (Rosa, 2013, p. 17). The desynchronization can be caused both by changes in the subjects and in acceleration of the programme (its nature, scope and length) and in the institutions, in terms of activities and participation requirements. On the institutional side, the acceleration takes place in the time regimes of the administrative, abstract systems (Rosa, 2013, p. 166). Desynchronization as a theoretical concept thus denotes the processes that lie outside and around the elements that create asynchrony.

Time as a signifier of belonging in higher education

Following and analysing how Jannie's, Esther's and Nanna's battles against temporal structures in their lives and in higher education reveal how dominant time and tempo have become as different timescapes and how linear succession and cyclicality intertwine and compete (Adam, 2008). A focus on acceleration of the education system combined with an interest in how students try to live up to notions of being capable as a student makes it possible to illuminate how time structures in a specific way frame student life. It shows how students become visible as people with psychosocial problems, how they are perceived in study programmes and how they experience themselves in relation to education. For example, delays often result in a number of exemptions, where both students and staff spend much time preparing and processing cases, which are often part of a very complicated set of rules that few students have insight into (cf. Chapter 8). The asynchronous students are hit hardest here because they lose the opportunities to make good decisions in terms of time and predictability. The time factor is partly expressed in the fact that the structural and administrative conditions for studying are constantly changing in nature, for example, through continuous education reforms, curriculum changes, frequent reorganization of administrative procedures, no permanent premises, etc. For the programmes, the time factor means that it becomes increasingly difficult to adapt the study conditions to a student who needs a semester with fewer activities. Asynchrony will thus mean a new way of sorting students, regardless of their academic level and potential in general.

Students' opportunities for and desire to engage in the activities and environment of the programme, together with interaction with fellow students, teachers and staff, are of great importance for their experience of identification and belonging in relation to the programme and thus their learning processes and academic success (Colley et al., 2003; Thomas, 2012; Wenger, 2004). Some students succeed without great difficulty in achieving a strong academic and social affiliation in their education and in creating meaning in student life. For other students, and especially for the asynchronous ones, participation will be made more difficult, and in many cases, they will have a more peripheral position as participants. In our analysis, it is the sorting dynamics linked to asynchrony, probably as much as students' specific psychosocial problems, that make it harder for them to feel belonging and identity as part of a larger student community.

Behind the current legitimate pedagogical text are neoliberal trends and reforms, changing the notion of student time and temporality, making time itself a competition parameter and a new sorting mechanism. Students experiencing and dealing with psychosocial problems have particular challenges conforming to these time structures, and they easily become, by way of time-oriented categories, so-called asynchronous students, designated as 'delayed.' Students who do not follow the institutional time structures are often not perceived as legitimate students, which shows how psychosocial problems make them unsuitable to the academic time tempo and time pressure. In this sense, time has become an important signifier of belonging and recognition, or of exclusion.

References

Adam, B. (2008). *The timescapes challenge: Engagement with the invisible temporal.* Leeds Talk Prose Timescapes Challenge.

Bengtsen, S. E., Sarauw, L. L., & Filippakou, O. (2021). In search of student time: Student temporality and the future university. In S. E. Bengtsen, S. Robinson, & W. Shumar (Eds.), *The university becoming. Perspectives from philosophy and social theory. Debating higher education: Philosophical perspectives* (Vol. 6, pp. 95–109). Springer.

Bennett, A., & Burke, P. J. (2017). Re/conceptualising time and temporality: An exploration of time in higher education. *Discourse: Studies in the Cultural Politics of Education, 39*(6), 913–925.

Bernstein, B. (2001). Pædagogiske koder og deres praksismodaliteter [Pedagogical codes and their modalities of practice]. In L. Chouliaraki & M. Bayer (Eds.), *Basil Bernstein, pædagogik, diskurs og magt* [*Basil Bernstein, pedagogy, discourse and power*] (pp. 69–93). Akademisk Forlag.

Bourdieu, P. (1996). *The state nobility: Elite schools in the field of power.* Polity Press.

Brooks, R., Abrahams, J., Gupta, A., Jayadeva, S., & Laztic, P. (2021). Higher education timescapes: Temporal understandings of students and learning. *Sociology.* https://doi.org/10.1177/0038038521996979

Burke, P. J., Bennett, A., Burgess, C., Gray, K., & Southgate, E. (2016). *Capability, belonging and equity in higher education: Developing inclusive approaches*. The University of Newcastle.

Burke, P. J., & Crozier, G. (2014). Higher education pedagogies: Gendered formation, mis-recognition and emotion. *Journal of Research in Gender Studies, 4*(2), 52–67.

Colley, H., David, J., Diment, K., & Tedder, M. (2003). Learning as becoming in vocational education and training: Class, gender and the role of vocational habitus. *Journal of Vocational Education & Training, 55*(4), 471–498.

Domina, T., Penner, A., & Penner, E. (2017). Categorical inequality: Schools as sorting machines. *Annual Review of Sociology, 43*, 311–330.

EU. (2015). *The ECTS users' guide*. Office for Official Publications of the European Communities.

Rosa, H. (2013). *Social acceleration: A new theory of modernity*. Columbia University Press.

Sarauw, L. L., & Madsen, S. R. (2016). *Studerende i en fremdriftstid: Prioriteter, valg og dilemmaer set i lyset af fremdriftsreformen: Analyser og tal fra landsdækkende spørgeskemaundersøgelse blandt 4.354 universitetsstuderende.* [*Students in a time of progress: Priorities, choices and dilemmas seen in the light of the progress reform: Analyses and figures from a nationwide questionnaire of 4354 university students*]. DPU, Århus University.

Sarauw, L. L., & Madsen, S. R. (2020). Higher education in the paradigm of speed: Student perspective on the risks of fast-track degree completion. *Learning and Teaching, 13*(1), 1–23.

Thomas, L. (2012). *Building student engagement and belonging in higher education at a time of change: Final report from the what works? Student retention & success programme*. Paul Hamley Foundation.

Wenger, E. (2004). *Praksisfællesskaber* [*Communities of practice*]. Hans Reitzels Forlag.

7 "If you don't feel at ease socially." Recognition, loneliness and communities in higher education

> *[I]f you don't feel that you belong somewhere, then it can be extremely difficult to focus on the academic part. It's as if some energy is taken from you. That's at least my experience. – If you don't feel at ease socially.*

This quote from one of the students in the Study Life Project, a female student of medicine, indicates several aspects of the impact of communities as a foundation for belonging in higher education. First, the feeling of belonging is important, and it is intertwined with the conditions for the academic work, and secondly, it provides feelings of comfort and safety which play an important role as an underlying foundation and driving force for learning processes. A sense of belonging is generally important to students, whether it relates to the academic domain, the social domain, the student's environment or the personal space (Ahn & Davis, 2020). Students are on a learning trajectory, in a continual process of 'becoming.' This process is dynamic and may take different and unexpected turns and, over time, be influenced by and influence the interacting factors of 'being' (who am I), 'becoming' (who will I be) and 'belonging' (how and where do I fit in) (Meehan & Howells, 2019). Of course, students are diverse and what motivates and nurtures one student's well-being may not have the same impact on another student.

Participation in and membership of communities and experiences of belonging are not static, once achieved or granted, and thereafter never to be lost. These are dynamic, fluid processes, which change over time and space (Gravett & Ajjawi, 2021), thus providing multiple perspectives to students' experiences of being, becoming and belonging. Some communities in higher education can be characterized as short-term, intensive working relationships arising from assignments or projects, while others are of longer duration and may include social and affective dimensions. Furthermore, the situated aspect of belonging to a community must not be overlooked, including the impact of space, artefacts and other physical dimensions of the contextual framework for student life and study communities.

The preceding chapter presented some of the barriers and obstacles students may encounter in their efforts to remain participants in their study communities, in terms of asynchrony, and time- and energy-consuming tasks to ensure the

DOI: 10.4324/9781003221029-7

foundation for continued studies. This chapter shows students' negotiations of the meaning of study communities and their importance, students' identity development related to (un)available and/or chosen communities and the processes of recognition or misrecognition involved in the learning trajectories into or out of communities. The chapter draws primarily on the accounts of two master's students, Louise and William, who participated in the Study Life Project and, through individual interviews and talks during visits to places of personal importance, gave us insights into their experiences, their battles and the communities affecting their lives as students. Louise is a 26-year-old student of social science who suffers from stress-related symptoms, which started in her third year, and William is a 31-year-old student of engineering who has a long history of battling with depression and grief due to deaths in his family. The two students have been chosen to illustrate two very different trajectories in higher education and the role communities play in their identity development. Their biographies are intertwined with their values, choices and actions, and through the differences in their individual experiences, some common traits emerge.

In this chapter, we draw on E. Wenger's social theory of learning in communities of practice (Wenger, 1998). In this understanding, practice, community, identity, meaning and learning are interconnected and mutually defining, and we understand the concept of community as a dynamic, continually changing entity, subject to the ongoing negotiation of meaning by its participants. The dynamics of belonging is further conceptualized with Antonsich's (2010) term for physical and emotional attachment, 'place-belongingness,' and his term 'politics of belonging' relating to collectivities and group membership, which may be granted or denied. We explore belonging as situated practice (Gravett & Ajjawi, 2021; Wenger, 1998), considering the influence of 'timescapes' (Bennett & Burke, 2018) on belonging and identity development. The students' negotiations of identity are intertwined with experiences of recognition and misrecognition, and in the analysis, we find the intersubjective patterns of recognition, namely love, justice/respect and solidarity (Honneth, 2006/1992), helpful in understanding and categorizing the phenomena we observe in the students' experiences.

Communities as a foundation for academic work

> *[O]ne of those girls celebrated her 25th birthday not long ago, and then you hear that many students from the class were there. And then I felt, it's okay I've sort of dumped them, but still it really quickly became a topic of conversation and if you are not part of it or do not talk about it with those people, then you can get the feeling that I'm not welcome here.*

Louise, quoted above, is in her fourth year of a master's programme in social science. She is unhappy as a student and has developed stress symptoms such as anxiety, headaches, dizziness and concentration problems due to a conflict with fellow students who previously were her closest friends and study group. In the quote, Louise explains her present position in relation to her former friends. She is no longer part of the group as she has chosen to withdraw from them, and she feels the social repercussions keenly, not just in relation to the girls in the group but also in relation to the rest of the class. She is afraid of being talked about behind her back because of the conflict. She does not even feel that her present position is at the periphery with opportunities for participation (Wenger, 1998) but rather outside the border of the social community. She perceives the study community as a network where everybody is in contact with her former friends, and she fears that anything she might say may be repeated to them.

> *And I strongly feel that because I dumped them, then I'm left with that feeling that it just excludes a lot of opportunities for me, in terms of talking to someone, because then I get to be careful. Now I also have to be careful with what I say to this and that person because they talk to them.*

The conflict is rooted in an incident involving the girls referred to in the quote. During a night out with these friends from the study group, one of the girls' boyfriends commented on Louise's hair and skin colour in a derogatory and racist manner, which shocked her and made her sad; but, she was even more disappointed that her friends did not see how this affected her and did not react and stand up for her.

> *[B]ut why didn't they do something or why didn't they say anything to him? Why did people just let this happen? . . . When you are silent in such a group situation, then you easily become like a co-executioner or a bit like an accomplice to the situation. I just think it was a mixture of being angry, disappointed with the situation because they simply could not understand what the problem was.*

The boyfriend's actions were offensive and the misrecognition and shock Louise felt were not seen or acknowledged by her close friends from whom she would expect reactions conforming to the patterns of love, justice and solidarity (Honneth, 2006/1992). The absence of understanding, respect and caring reactions towards her was experienced as another and even worse violation, emphasized by the terms 'co-executioner' and 'accomplice.' This experience eventually led to the complexity of Louise's present psychosocial problems. The situation seems to have triggered previous experiences from Louise's childhood.

> *[S]omehow I feel a little set back [in time], I feel like I'm sitting in that primary school class again and I'm like seven or eight years old, and people are saying "Well, why have you got curly hair? Why?"*
>
> *. . . because now I experienced something that is so radically or completely different from anything I have ever experienced. And it has somehow recalled some old feelings, I kind of feel that's it, it's some old feelings in a new context.*

In her school years, Louise was not a member of one particular group of friends but had relations with all the groups. She moved away from her home town to study, and at university, she becomes a member of a study group, which develops into a closely knit group of friends that do everything together. Belonging to a group is a new experience for Louise, and she is unprepared for the above incident, which recalls all the embodied experiences and feelings that are part of her biography; but in this case, they create a very different effect and stronger reactions because the incident takes place in a context where she does not expect this kind of behaviour.

> *Yes, but just in a completely different context because as much as I recognize the feeling, there is still the difference that, well, I may have been harassed as a child, but I had at least someone in my class that I could find to talk to, someone who was actually there for me, but I don't feel I've got that here now. Now I feel I'm alone with it, and it makes me maybe a bit scared of – reaching out to people, or – opening myself up to them, because they used to actually be quite close to me, and we used to have a really good time together, and then it really just hurts a lot that those you had the best time with are the ones who have hurt you the most.*

This has resulted in her social withdrawal from the study community as a whole and has also led to postponement of her exams. The choice to un-belong to a community may be productive (Guyotte et al., 2019), and Louise's choice to separate herself from the study group and work alone was indeed made to reduce her feelings of stress and anxiety and provide a productive study situation, yet it turned out to have the opposite effect. Louise's understanding of this situation is that the choices she has made to work alone in an otherwise collaborative learning environment, to take subjects in a different order than is usual and to postpone some exams – and to be open about it – are breaking some of the 'rules' of the study culture. She disrupts the traditional trajectory in higher education, thus laying herself open to being interpreted as 'non-traditional' or perhaps lacking the ability to perform on time. Her ways of dealing with time and study progression reflect her 'timescape' (Bennett & Burke, 2018), that is, a combination of her previous experience of education and relationships, her anxiety and ongoing speculations about the sociocultural context of her studies, her loneliness and her efforts to manage the total complexity. In doing so, she is, however, no longer certain that she is considered a legitimate participant of the study community, and learning trajectories have been closed to her in terms of collaboration and socialization with other students.

> *So I actually feel that when I had announced that now I really wanted to try to write a project [alone], it was a final thing and it also meant that I gave up everything else that had to do with other people.*

In Louise's understanding there is no going back, and she sees no possibilities for negotiating new or alternative trajectories for her into the study community again. When she no longer feels that there are other students who depend on her to do her part, or that her contribution is important to others, it becomes difficult to maintain her motivation to study and go to lectures: "it got to be too much for me, with the non-existent relationships that were there in the programme."

When she occasionally does attend classes, she feels that she must start from scratch regarding her social position and relationships in the class, and from being secure in her identity as a student and feeling at home in the class, she now has to negotiate her behaviour and question every aspect of it. She tells about an experience of physical exclusion in the classroom. She was the first to enter and sit down and afterwards several students from her cohort entered and they all positioned themselves in the opposite row. The situation was very uncomfortable, and she wondered if she was being harassed. Their act of not joining her imposed a physical divide, which led to Louise's emotional reaction and interpretation of the incident as a physical rejection and exclusion from the group. The rejection was experienced as an act of misrecognition; there was no solidarity with her (Honneth, 2006/1992).

This situation means that when Louise is at the university, she feels that she becomes physically (and socially) constrained, staying in the classroom during breaks or going to the less crowded corridors to avoid the other students, as she no longer seems to know how to interact with them.

> *I think, in relation to the place itself, being here on a daily basis, I'm probably not that good at leaving the room, for example when we have a break. I'm more likely to sit in my seat a lot, and then those thoughts often come back to me. And I kind of get stuck in the situation somehow. It's a bit uncomfortable, it's a little insecure. What should I do now? Who should I talk to now? Should I talk to anyone at all? And all that stuff is what's been bothering me.*

With reference to Antonsich's (2010) concept of place-belongingness, Louise does not feel 'at home' in the classroom any more, there is no sense of security, but instead discomfort and negative emotional and bodily reactions. Further, when there is no sense of place-belonging, the result is in Louise's case an enhanced sense of loneliness, which may further add to her motivational and mental health problems (Antonsich, 2010). In Louise's account, the feeling of loneliness seems to have reinforced the problems she has experienced. Another aspect of belongingness is mastering the language, the specific discourse, and knowing the codes and their interpretation as an important aspect of a sense of belonging to a place or a community. In Louise's case, the feeling of exclusion and her consequent loss of place-belongingness lead to a destabilization of her sense of mastery of the cultural codes of the specific context, illustrated by her insecurity related to leaving the classroom during breaks and socializing with other students.

From a recognition perspective, the loss of her closest friends relates to the first pattern of recognition, 'love,' and means that Louise loses the feeling of emotional acceptance and appreciation from the group that was part of her identity.

Her feeling of being disrespected by the group of friends and the ensuing social discomfort and confusion may in Honneth's framework be understood as a result of reduced self-confidence. Furthermore, in addition to the third pattern of recognition, 'solidarity,' the second pattern, 'justice/respect,' is at play in the experience of exclusion demonstrated when the students physically distance themselves from Louise, which is a form of symbolic rejection indicating denied membership (politics of belonging) and disrespect. When one meets disrespect from the surrounding community, which should respect one as a valued member, one's own self-respect may be jeopardized.

Being in the physical environment, 'the teaching context,' causes various bodily reactions in Louise; she feels cold all the time "even though I have three layers of clothes on I still feel cold," and she has problems with headaches and dizziness and concentration difficulties. Louise is seeing a therapist regularly to work on the problems, and even though the class-related physical environment triggers negative emotions and reactions, Louise tries as part of the homework from her therapist to go to the study's social space on campus, which is open every other Wednesday with cake and coffee on offer. She goes there bringing a book, her computer, etc., "so that people would not wonder why I am there." The assignment from the therapist is to practise reaching out to others socially, and Louise feels that it works for her to act in the situation and save the emotional ponderings until she gets home. However, back home she is completely exhausted from the effort and must deal with new speculations and ponderings about the interactions she managed to carry out. In this case, the room designated for relaxation and social encounters across the cohorts is used as a therapeutic tool to support Louise's road to recovery, a way to ease her way back into a study-related social community and practice her interpersonal skills about which she is uncertain at this stage, as indicated in the quote. In other words, she practices 'doing belonging' (Bell in Antonsich, 2010). However, even here Louise feels situated at the periphery and is not even sure that she is considered a legitimate participant (Wenger, 1998), which is why she makes sure she brings her legitimizing props (book, computer).

Louise is constantly negotiating the study community, its social dimensions and the physical spaces to find ways to deal with her emotional reactions to her experiences of misrecognition and her psychosocial challenges.

The role of community in renegotiating identity

Louise's perceived or experienced peripheral position does not offer her opportunities to take an active role in co-creating the study culture and its values. She has no influence on the culture and values, but they occupy an important place in Louise's negotiations of her understanding of the study community. In her analysis of the study community, she finds that to be a student you must make yourself visible and interesting to the teachers and to the other students and display a great deal of energy. In class, you must make yourself academically interesting to the teacher to be recognized, for instance by presenting unusual, innovative project ideas that the teacher thinks are interesting or has never thought of as a problem. Out of class, the study community has a virtual life on Facebook, and here students who make an extra effort for the community are promoted, for instance if they post that they are baking cakes for the students to buy and will then donate the profits to charity. This kind of action receives positive attention and recognition from other students and is part of the politics of belonging which Louise finds it hard to adhere to because of the underlying self-promotion:

> *I don't know, I feel you have to be a certain type, or have a certain attitude, and that you have to make a lot of noise, . . . that's the kind of ideal. If other students don't make noise for you, then you make noise yourself by saying "look at me," "look what I've done" and so on. And I think I have always had a hard time with that.*

It is important to be visible and call attention to yourself to be seen and acknowledged as part of the study community. Being no longer part of the community, Louise analyses the values from a more critical perspective, and in her reflection, she finds that they are not compatible with her own values and preferred behaviour. Her efforts are focused on not being seen and not standing out. Belonging to this community would therefore require a different kind of practice and behaviour from Louise and probably a homogenization of identity (Mann, 2005) which she at this point distances herself from. Un-belonging to the study community becomes part of Louise's process of "becoming" and her renegotiation of identity (Gravett & Ajjawi, 2021). But at the same time, the lack of relationships and place-belongingness in the study context comes at a price and causes further stress and uncertainty: "I feel there's no safe place in the group called 'study group.'" Louise must therefore turn to other kinds of communities to experience recognition, acknowledgement and identity confirmation. Amongst these communities is her part-time student job, which she characterizes as 'routine,' 'safe' and 'predictable,' and which thus has a favourable impact on Louise's state of mind: "Yes, the constant thoughts going round in my head, I get rid of them . . . in a way. I'm definitely able to relax a lot more in my head when I'm at work, when I'm with my friends, my family."

When Louise is with family and friends, there is no need for her to think about her behaviour and reactions; this also applies to being with her colleagues at work as they know her and know what to expect. Furthermore, at work, Louise's contribution is needed, she is instructed in what to do, there are few risks of doing anything wrong, and if she does, she corrects it. In addition to being a safe community, work is a place where Louise experiences recognition and respect in terms of both the 'justice' and 'solidarity' patterns (Honneth, 2006/1992). She is seen and acknowledged as a person in her own right and her contribution is expected and valued. Belonging to this community is one of the strong reasons why Louise decides against taking leave from or dropping out of her programme, which she is tempted to do, since she would not be able to continue in the student job if she did not remain registered as an active student.

Louise's lack of self-confidence leads to a fear of having become *'socially awkward'* in general; so, to 'test' herself in that respect, she at some point independently takes the initiative to seek confirmation of her self-efficacy by participating in meetings in networks that are new to her and not related to her study context. Here, she experiences warm welcomes and an interest in her as a person, and she has no problems with her interpersonal social skills or feelings of insecurity. She finds she is met with respect as a person of interest in her own right, as in the second pattern of recognition, 'justice,' and is thus able to feel vindicated as her self-esteem is positively confirmed.

Even though the study community in Louise's understanding does not offer her educational trajectories she feels able to take at this point, and although she is tempted to drop out, she is still genuinely interested in the subject areas that she had chosen to study, including topics such as community, ethnicity and culture. Her personal experience with communities and being an outsider is one of the reasons why she chose this particular programme in the first place:

I knew very well it was a subject that had something to do with people and how to study society in a contemporary context, how we humans in general interact, individually, in groups, differences, similarities, that's all extremely relevant to me. And I also think that there is probably something personal in it again, because I know what it is like when you are not part of that group, but then also vice versa look at what happens when you are part of a group? And what about the others who are outside, in one way or another? So about communities and what defines or what decides that you're in a community and what doesn't, who is in and who is out, in reality? I find it really exciting to look at that, so I think that was the idea that made me end up in social science.

In Louise's situation where she searches for communities to match her values, interests and experiences, podcasts on her academic interests and related subject areas become another way for Louise to seek a community to identify with and belong to.

At the moment I listen a lot to podcasts actually, so I don't know if it's also a way to look for a community where specific topics are addressed, because I get so absorbed in or I am so interested in communities and ethnicity and culture and different cultural backgrounds, it's something that really interests me a lot. And then I found this podcast where these exact topics are treated, and that's something I do quite a lot. Actually, when I look at my circle of friends and the people I regularly talk to, it's like they all have some background or other. I have a friend for example, her mother is a Greenlander, her father is Danish, and I'm also myself, that is, I have a Danish father, my mother is from Ghana, so there is also something there. So, if I look closely at my circle of friends, I realize it is a theme that repeats itself, and is something that interests me a lot, and the inequalities around [us]. How it can sometimes be a disadvantage to have a certain appearance or a certain name and so on, which I talk a lot with my friends about, because it is something that they have each experienced in different ways. So it may well be that I am cultivating some sense of community in some way.

Louise's personal life story and experiences with ethnicity and inclusion/exclusion here become apparent as intertwined with her academic interest and curiosity and her search for a community to belong to. Louise reflects that the imagined community of the podcast mirrors the community of her friends in that they have some of the same characteristics regarding ethnicity as well as similar experiences regarding inequalities and disadvantages, together with a common interest in discussing these and related topics. In this community, Louise finds recognition and a sense of belonging without having to battle for it. Her conflicts and crises have forced her to renegotiate her identity, who she is and wants to be, and, in this respect, the subjects she is studying support her process of 'becoming.' Because the subject area is so closely related to her biography, it plays an important role as both a constant factor in the complexity of her life and at the same time a driver for her identity development.

Louise has experienced the stigma of being pointed out as different from the norm, which led to a vicious circle of experiences of un-belonging in the study community and self-reinforcing psychosocial problems. The process involves continual thoughts and reflections on the study context and its values, the actions of her previous friends, her own role and reactions and her longing to be part of the broader study community. In Louise's negotiations of belonging and her identity formation, the communities outside the programme are where she finds virtual and physical place-belongingness as well as recognition, allowing her to renegotiate her identity. Her personal history and previous experiences shape her perception of the incidents and are both intertwined with and further enhance her academic interest. Louise chooses communities that she finds supportive in her processes of negotiating her 'being' and 'becoming,' and as we have seen, the study community does not qualify in that respect.

A journey towards a supportive community

For William, it is a very different story, which eventually, after a long series of battles, reveals the positive impact of recognition and solidarity in a learning community.

William is a master's student who has suffered from grief and depression since high school due to the sudden illness and death of his mother, followed by the death of his father a few years later. His depression has led to concentration problems and, when we first meet him, he feels as if he is in a constant daze, which makes it difficult for him to contemplate his future. Ever since before high school, his greatest wish has been to study psychology, but the recurring periods of depression resulted in prolonged absences from high school, several sick leaves and delayed exams. His grades were affected, and he could not achieve the average necessary to study psychology at university. Instead, he opted for a vocational education that suited him well under the circumstances, with physical activities in the open air and not too much reading. However, his battles for his desired education were not over.

Having suffered a physical injury during his studies that prevented him from taking a physical exam, he was not offered an alternative form of examination. The rigidness of the educational system thus prevented him from taking the final exam of his vocational education, and consequently, this entire educational endeavour was wasted. William could not complete the programme and had to start all over again to create a new educational trajectory, this time in a bachelor's programme. When we first meet William, he is in his last semester of this programme.

Due to the asynchronicity caused by the delays (see also Chapter 6), William has felt lonely in his study environments in relation to the other students. In high school, he was considered the odd one out because of his absences and was called '*guest of the week*' by his classmates when he managed to attend. There was little compassion or understanding of his situation by his peers and consequently no help to be gained, or in Honneth's terminology, there was no emotional attention or social appreciation from his classmates. In his studies after high school, his absences meant that he did not feel that he could contact the students he had previously studied with and ask them for help. William felt that "*they would not invest time in me.*" In neither case is he positioned as a full member of the study community, nor is he recognized in terms of the patterns of 'solidarity,' as someone whose contribution is expected and valued (Honneth, 2006/1992). His loneliness is both of a social and academic nature since it is not possible for him to establish relationships where he can discuss subject-related issues and negotiate meaning together with other students (Wenger, 1998). William has therefore basically needed to manage his learning trajectories by himself and independently. Consequently, he makes an effort to be knowledgeable about the rules and regulations and not just rely on the system to take care of him. His strategy has always been to inform the study administration about his situation at any given time, to make sure that he is recognized by the system and to get any help available. Nevertheless, he was once forgotten by the administration, which almost cost him an exam, were it not for his own alertness and intervention.

William's battles to finish a programme and get a degree are related to his wish to be able to support himself financially, that is, to be no longer dependent on the state grant, which he supplements through part-time jobs. He wants to be settled, have fixed routines, and have his own place. One effect of his depression is his difficulty in recognizing and ascertaining his own competencies and qualifications, and as his bachelor's degree does not provide him with a title, he finds that he has to continue to take a master's degree, so that he does not have 'to fight even more,' but can rely on the title of the master's degree to vouch for his qualifications.

Time for becoming

In our last interview, William is in the final year of his master's degree, and he feels that at the age of 31 he has finally reached 'the other side':

> *Now I can put it away and make this work – start over again. This is the end of my education. . . . I do not want any more – I am now so old and should have*

> *finished six years ago the way I planned it. . . . I can put my history behind me – my repeated attempts at getting an education.*

William is 'on the other side' in the sense that he is less marked by or likely to fall into a depressive mode, not easily shaken emotionally, and getting good marks. He states that he knows who he is ('being') and has developed strategies for dealing with it when he experiences signs of oncoming depressive moods and he has no prolonged absences from the programme. Furthermore, he has devised learning strategies for dealing with his concentration problems, and this is reflected in his academic results, which are back at the same level as before the depression, that is, he is getting top grades. Referring to the concept of 'timescapes' (Bennett & Burke, 2018), we see that William is battling with accepting his own timescape, when he says 'should have finished six years ago,' a statement that reflects the general sociocultural expectations regarding the traditional student trajectory. He is in other words not 'on time.' Furthermore, a remaining issue from the depression is that William still has difficulty in seeing himself in a future perspective and has only a short horizon, "I cannot see for instance five years ahead." The missing time perspective is combined with a belief in his own lack of competency and influences his processes of 'becoming.' He claims to suffer a lot from 'imposter syndrome' and has difficulty imagining himself in a job. Getting the master's degree will help, but he feels that he is 'cheating' his way through and seeks confirmation in several places. Despite having considerable experience of volunteer work and student jobs, William believes his lack of confidence will not change until he has secured his first paid job, the type of recognition that society at large accepts as a sign of competence and value.

At this stage of his education, William enjoys being in sync with the programme and the class of students he started with. As indicated, he is, however, now considerably older than his classmates, who have come directly from high school and their bachelor's programme: "At times I feel old. . . . Then you're a bit like an old grandpa." He sometimes feels a little out of place as an 'adult' in relation to the other students. By virtue of his traumas, which he feels have aged him considerably, he also feels much older than some of his teachers. Even though William is now in the eyes of the educational system 'on time' with his class, the context means that he cannot ignore his own personal timescape (Bennett & Burke, 2018) and how it influences his identity.

William helps others when he can, and because of his own problems, he has, as mentioned earlier, made a point of getting thoroughly acquainted with the educational system and its rules, and thus becomes the 'go-to guy' when students or others need help: "It happens quite a lot that international students and others who are a bit lost gravitate towards me. I help them out, and it takes so little of my time, and it helps them so much."

His biography is reflected in this, both in terms of helping those 'who are a bit lost' and in terms of noticing those who may be at the periphery or outside the border of the community (Wenger), such as international students, and he acts in a manner that recognizes them as legitimate and valuable members of the community (Honneth, 2006/1992), thus facilitating their learning trajectories.

Class culture as imperative for learning

He credits the education, that is, the fact that he was allowed admission to the master's programme, and his small class (15 students) with some part of his positive state of recovery. William states that the class is important because of the interaction and mutual support; they talk about everything including emotions and William feels that he is a respected member of the group and that he contributes in a positive way to both the class climate and their academic discussions: "of course, some [students] have to work harder than others, but it is up to the class to carry people through, because we are in it together."

In a Wengerian perspective, William's quote can be interpreted as an indication that he feels that the class is a community with a joint enterprise and mutual engagement, where meaning is negotiated and a joint repertoire created (Wenger, 1998). In William's view, each of the students is responsible for contributing to their common goal of learning and both social and academic aspects are of great importance in that effort since they are responsible not only for their own learning but for the learning of the others in the class, as indicated in 'it is up to the class to carry people through.' The study community is here presented as a positive and constructive learning space of situated social practice (Gravett & Ajjawi, 2021). William explains that they are good at sharing with each other, and they have a strong sense of solidarity in his class. They share notes, for instance, if someone was unable to attend lectures or tutorials, which William has never experienced in his previous studies: "Very nice that people back you up if you can't be there yourself."

Furthermore, the mutual expectations and appreciation of each other's contributions towards the common goal may be interpreted as a sign of Honneth's third pattern of recognition, 'solidarity,' in the expression of reciprocal respect and belief in the other's capabilities. William further describes a community feeling and a class climate where it is safe to ask questions, which supports his positive development: "You do not feel stupid if you ask, because we are all interdisciplinary and have different strengths."

At the same time, William himself is also an important driver for creating just such an environment, for example by initiating discussions with the teacher in which the rest of the class gradually takes part, thus creating what he describes as "a good learning environment." With reference to Antonsich's concepts of belonging, William himself thus benefits from a feeling of 'place-belongingness,' and he also actively strives to create this for the rest of the class, as well as working on the 'politics of belonging' to create an inclusive environment. In William's opinion, the class culture is therefore imperative for supporting learning.

> *The culture in the classroom does more for the whole and more for the quality of what is done or learned than the basic teaching or lectures. . . . The culture is, when people are in doubt, we talk about it. Sometimes, we take over the lecture and discuss instead. That makes for a better study environment.*

William's understanding of the student community in his programme is that it is a dynamic entity and established through and dependent on an ongoing process of participation, contribution and negotiation in which students and teachers are all acknowledged as equally valuable agents/actors. The concept of community is that it is an ongoing process through which class culture is created and it continually creates a supportive learning environment, where both students and teachers demonstrate agency. In William's understanding, even the building where the education takes place has a positive significance and further supports the creation of a fruitful and transparent learning community: "It is a public space that invites a feeling of community, invites discussion – you can see what everyone is doing – there are no secrets."

In William's case, the education affords the possibility of active involvement, and the recognition and respect he receives from the other students and the teachers strengthens his identity as a legitimate, full participant in the programme. He is active in creating a study culture and environment that in many ways takes into account the things William has missed and had to battle with during his own educational experiences.

William's trajectory and final positive experiences of belonging have resulted in stronger knowledge about who he is ('being') and although it is difficult for him to imagine who he will or can be professionally in the future ('becoming'), in the final year of his master's he begins to form specific ideas of what kind of work he would prefer, which is another sign of William's recovery process.

Recognition, loneliness and communities

In these accounts, we see a number of different battles with other students as adversaries, as well as battles for and with fellow students. The battles take different forms but the main issues at stake in these battles are to remain in academia and keep one's position as a student in terms of being part of a study community and as a formally recognized student in the study programme ('belonging'), to progress in one's educational trajectory, and support one's identity development ('becoming'). In both accounts, the students' processes of coming to terms with who they are ('being') and who they wish to be are closely intertwined with processes of belonging and un-belonging. The individual person's relationship with a community is closely related to negotiation and development of identity and the stories show the importance of a community and its positive influence on the feelings of well-being and self-efficacy, which are the result of being a respected and valued contributing member. However, they also show the loneliness and experiences of misrecognition and exclusion when one cannot join a community. It is a vulnerable position to be on the periphery of the study community. Negotiations of belonging to communities are fundamental to student 'being' and 'becoming,' as a foundation for identity formation, self-esteem and confidence. The battles for belonging and the negotiations of identity in the two accounts illustrate the processes of being and becoming as also a search for – and a longing for – one's own recognition of oneself.

In both accounts, it is evident that to be recognized as a student one has to look out for oneself and make an effort to be visible, to be seen, which emphasizes the individualizing aspects of higher education. The paradox here is that it is important to stand out as an individual to receive recognition from and admission to the study community, but if one stands out in a socioculturally non-acceptable way such as by not following the universal educational timeline but one's own timescape, access to study communities can be difficult, if not impossible. The concept of 'timescape' here captures the complexity of the meaning of the individual student's biography intertwined with the student's dealing with time, context and situated practice.

For different reasons and at different times in their respective history, both Louise and William had a feeling of being outside study communities, and in the present situation, they both have to individually and independently find relevant, sustainable ways forward. Their interest in their subjects plays an important role in driving their identity development and their respective biographies are strongly reflected in the actions they take. Rather than being alone, they both become active by joining new communities. Through their agency, they each manage to turn their situation around, either by finding compensatory communities or by creating inclusive learning communities. The communities opted for provide positive recognition and are, in varying degrees, related to their academic interests.

The two accounts show that psychosocial problems are not indicators of a static problematic situation or condition; they develop and change according to, for example, their environment, society, the institution, the study context and may be related to enablers and barriers to negotiations of 'being' and 'becoming' through opportunities of belonging to a community. Here, processes of recognition and misrecognition play an important part.

References

Ahn, M. Y., & Davis, H. H. (2020). Four domains of students' sense of belonging to university. *Studies in Higher Education, 45*(3), 622–634. Retrieved August 11, 2021, from https://discovery.ucl.ac.uk/id/eprint/10100833/3/Ahn_final%20accepted%20four%20domains%20SHE%2026102018.pdf

Antonsich, M. (2010). Searching for belonging – an analytical framework. *Geography Compass, 4*(6), 644–659.

Bennett, A., & Burke, P. J. (2018). Re/conceptualizing time and temporality: An exploration of time in higher education. *Discourse: Studies in the Cultural Politics of Education, 39*(6), 913–925.

Gravett, K., & Ajjawi, R. (2021). Belonging as situated practice. *Studies in Higher Education.* https://doi.org/10.1080/03075079.2021.1894118

Guyotte, K. W., Flint, M. A., & Latopolski, K. S. (2019). Cartographies of belonging: Mapping nomadic narratives of first-year students. *Critical Studies in Education.* https://doi.org/10.1080/17508487.2019.1657160

Honneth, A. (2006/1992). *Kamp om anerkendelse. Sociale konflikters moralske Grammatik* [*The struggle for recognition: The moral grammar of social conflicts*]. Hans Reitzel.

Mann, S. J. (2005). Alienation in the learning environment: A failure of community? *Studies in Higher Education, 30*(1), 43–55.

Meehan, C., & Howells, K. (2019). In search of the feeling of 'belonging' in higher education: Undergraduate students transition into higher education. *Journal of Further and Higher Education, 43*(10), 1376–1390. https://doi.org/10.1080/0309877X.2018.1490702

Wenger, E. (1998). *Communities of practice: Learning, meaning, and identity.* Cambridge University Press.

8 "I see it as an extra job I have." Students' extra work in making higher education accessible

> *I sent in my medical records, a statement from my doctor, and I had a statement from a specialist due to my PTSD. . . . So I really pulled out all the stops to apply for that extension for my master's thesis. . . . I think the first time I applied for an extension for the thesis, it took me three months to collect all of this material. . . . and for three months I did not look at my thesis at all. . . . I cried my eyes out every time I had to write the written statement, so I had to put it away and then pick it up again and then I would start to cry again because I had to explain what happened to someone in writing . . . . and suddenly after having put it away for forever, then I had to go into it, AND I had to make someone understand it, AND it was also the thing that had to ensure my entire education. So a lot was at stake and at the same time I had to really get into the trauma. . . . it really was a difficult time*

Caroline was in a serious road accident as a child and the doctors told her it was a miracle that she is functioning so well today. Caroline got all the way to her master's thesis until a sudden new illness made her look into the medical records, mentioned earlier, from her childhood accident. As a child, her parents yelled at her when she tried to bring the accident up. At the final part of her master's, she now realized that she had to deal with the trauma she suffers from not being allowed to talk about her accident. It became crucial for her to find treatment for the trauma in order to move on in her life. She then figured that it was better to do this while studying rather than waiting until she had completed her degree and was supposed to look for work. She rationalized that it would be better for society to treat the trauma while she was on a lower public allowance (educational state grant). Then she could fulfil the role of being a good citizen and help society. But as Caroline explains in the quote above, it ended up requiring considerable time, energy and emotional strain to create the physical, temporal, financial and emotional space for being both a student doing her master's thesis and a student recovering from a trauma created in her childhood.

In the research project, we heard numerous stories like this one from Caroline. Stories about the work students had to do finding and putting time and energy into seeking help, support and someone to talk to, activating support and

DOI: 10.4324/9781003221029-8

help systems, going to doctors, writing waiver letters, hoping for a waiver to be approved, seeking extra funding and while doing that contemplating in general about their status of belonging in higher education. As for Caroline above, that affected them psychosocially in numerous ways. It particularly activated emotional work about student identity and whether they were living up to the norms of being "proper" students (Burke & Crozier, 2014) or not, doing something else than taking care of fulfilling the criteria for their academic work.

In that sense, having a disability or experiencing psychosocial difficulties as a student implied spending a great deal of extra time and energy on trying to reconnect, recalibrate and reconstitute their bodily, mental and emotional state into some idea of what counted as higher education standards, norms and 'properness.' Educational difficulties intersected with processes of going to psychiatrists, psychologists, student counsellors, mentoring programmes, doctors, priests, administrative staff, the local council, etc. Consequently, the students we interviewed spend much time in different kinds of systems and often after discovering the possibilities for special pedagogical support by chance. Even gaining the needed support was often described as a long and exhausting battle of practical work, emotional strain and challenged self-belief about worthiness and recognition as a legitimate student. We became curious about the dualities contained in the students' experience of activating and working the help and support systems and how this pointed towards exploring how ideas, discourses or norms of properness were being re-negotiated as criteria of belonging (Davies, 2000). The work students had to do in systems both within and outside higher education was work on demonstrating and illustrating ways to adhere to institutionalized logics of how a real, normal, and proper student acted, talked, walked, worked, performed and participated. Further, we found that this additional form of work emerged as a powerful theme in our interviews.

Students' extra work as reworking accessibility

When we listened to their stories, learning about the obstacles they had to overcome, we were immediately impressed by their willpower and determination when faced with what were often referred to as hostile systems. Surprisingly, their psychosocial problems did not develop into academic problems. On the contrary, immersion into a subject could often work as a form of refuge or be a place to feel acknowledged. Instead, more complex processes of in- and exclusion were taking place without any general pattern of decisive factors for their feelings of being troubled, delayed or disconnected from the social and professional communities in their department. In many cases, it was complex entanglements of biographical trajectories with higher education norms, structures and cultures that produced their subjective experience of need for help and support. In other cases, biographical experiences intertwined with sudden accidents such as concussion, death in the family, bad experiences with exams and pressure, or even forms of racism from fellow students at a private social gathering (see also Chapter 7). A mutual factor, however, was the feeling of walking a tightrope of higher education rules, norms and culture. That could involve being delayed and pressured on time for completion or experiencing psychosocial problems related to feelings of being pushed out to the sidelines. Entanglements of difficulties could also be related to structural processes of marginalization due to e.g. disability, diseases, psychiatric diagnoses, or dyslexia. All in all, these factors created difficulties for participating in their studies. As stated in the quote from Caroline, the time, energy and effort were not only a matter of implementing a piece of practical work. They had substantial implications for the process of identity formation and the emotional states, and seemed to challenge subjective self-understanding of belonging to education and society. It was surprising that despite a well-developed public healthcare system and a relatively well-functioning special pedagogical support system for students with a documented disability or functional impairment, the different forms of help and support they turned to seemed to produce subtle feelings of being separated out as special cases deviating from an idealized generalized student figure. Furthermore, the process of being in need of help was mostly associated with a feeling of shame for not being strong, resilient or robust enough.

In the interviews, students elaborated in detail about the practical dimension of the ways they navigated and coordinated institutional systems. This made us turn towards institutional ethnography and the work of sociologist Dorothy Smith and her concept of work knowledge. Drawing on the work of Smith, we started exploring how the everyday life of being a student involved in help and support systems was organized and coordinated within distinct forms of contemporary ruling relations (Smith, 2005). Later in the process, this made us aware of the work of Stephanie Hannam-Swain (2018), who, on the basis of her own experiences as a disabled PhD student, conceptualizes the practical dimensions of the extra work she must do as *additional labour*.

When we worked with student perspectives and emergent listening as a methodological principle (cf. Chapter 3), it was important that the exploration of ruling did not start in presumptions about what caused student difficulties. Instead, we approached the students' stories in a grounded manner, taking a decisive standpoint towards their everyday experiences and listening for the ways their practical work was linked to institutional rules of logic or what Smith conceptualizes as extra-local ruling relations (Smith, 2005, p. 49). This is an approach that "aims to go beyond what people know to find out how and what they are doing is connected with others' doings in ways they cannot see" (Smith, 2005, p. 225). The feeling of being punished for being sick, disabled, delayed or recovering from an illness was in that sense at the forefront of the students' experience of a problematic situation, but the ways students work, coordinated with others elsewhere such as professionals, administrative systems, educational or psychiatric institutions, came to constitute the object of our inquiry, where the issue was what kinds of organization of activities were taken for granted.

Conceptualizing the notion of work

Smith operates with a generous concept of work "as everything done by people that takes time and effort, that they mean to do, that is done under definite conditions and with whatever means and tools, and that they may have to think about" (Smith, 2005, pp. 151–152). This generous concept of work includes unpaid, unseen or invisible work within institutionalized forms of ruling. As Smith points out, obtaining a grade requires much more than reading literature, doing assignments or going to lectures:

> *We don't usually think of getting to class or the library as part of students' work (and, hence, part of the work producing the university as an everyday actuality).*
>
> (Smith, 2005, p. 152)

Following Smith's notion of work as social activities, the valuation of activities and subsequent coordinating of subjectivities is predominantly created within language in terms of ideas, concepts, theories and everyday talk, but is deeply integrated or manifested in the distribution of real activities without a body/mind divide (Smith, 2005, pp. 80–81). The ontology is that the social as taking part in institutional activities is to be understood as people coordinating activities in which language plays an essential part. As elaborated later, this was paramount in the ways students experienced the textual representation of their capabilities as students in applications for e.g. waivers or a disability allowance or in the gathering of documentation. In that sense, student participation in institutionalized forms of organizing and coordinating activities, which they turned to for help, treatment, clarification, recovery, financial support or avoiding rule-based forced resignations, was often based on textual forms of representation with considerable effect on how student belonging was negotiated. Furthermore, as Smith writes, participation in institutional activities, such as the gender or disabled divide, can be learned as something given or even talked about but in a sense of being "the problem that has no name"[1], which requires the development of a new language to talk about these doings and the real consequences of the effect it causes (Smith, 2005, pp. 78–79). Related to this, in a political neoliberal and capitalist economy, activities are bearers of a value differentiation relative to the understanding of the activities' financial contribution. In this regime, what is perceived as slowness, being delayed or being dependent on others or governmental subsidies can become a subtle and explicit symbol of economic deficits. Furthermore, as illustrated in Chapters 5, 6, and 7, these time and energy consuming activities are associated with shame and misrecognition. Nevertheless, this kind of work was understood as a necessary condition for most of the students in the research project with psychosocial problems, functional impairment or disabilities to produce and uphold an everyday actuality as a university student.

The empirical grounding

This was also the case for Beate, a student of the humanities with varying experiences of being a student. Her first three years as a philosophy student are described as a time of joy. She felt at home in the abstract subject, loved the academic discussions and being surrounded by 'fellow geeks.' But after having a bad experience at an examination she feels excluded from the programme and in a state of severe shame. She recalls feeling surrounded by shame, alone and outside in the dark. In the interview, Beate is troubled by the fact that the university system seems so indifferent to her well-being. She rhetorically asks why nobody from the administration calls her up to ask how she is doing, having suddenly failed the same exam twice after doing really well in her other exams and assignments. Beate touches upon the fact that students in higher education by tradition are left on their own without a traditional school class as a supportive framework and the lack of a teacher to be observant of and to monitor a pupil's well-being. Following Smith's notion of work, Beate indicates a specific higher education organization and coordination of study activities, where the handling of the social, relational and programme structure outside the format of the lecture is mostly work left to the students to do themselves. This also concerns the emotional spill-over effects of participating in often strongly affective performative spaces such as exams. After a difficult period where Beate feels distanced from the university and too ashamed to return and "look the teachers in the eyes," she instead chooses to follow another interest of hers, namely the study of religion, and therefore decides to leave philosophy and the specific university. Unfortunately, in the new programme there is a lack of social cohesion and "not enough geeks" who want to participate in extracurricular activities after lectures. It is difficult to find a position when entering an academically based community and hard to make new friends. As she explains in the interview, she ends up struggling to find a place to develop a sound study identity. Her mental condition worsens, and she ends up undergoing psychiatric treatment, which she has done previously in her life, and by chance she also discovers the possibility to be assigned special pedagogical support with a student counsellor and mentor.

When the mental illness takes control, she rarely sleeps. That affects her in many ways. By contrast, in her periods of well-being, she does very well academically. The consequence of becoming a delayed student due to periods of sickness and stress is that she must frequently write applications for waivers and for extra financial support. During the interview, Beate describes this work as hidden and shameful but also an integrated and necessary part of her work and battle for maintaining a position as a legitimate student institutionally, financially and subjectively regarding her identity and self-belief in the future. She describes the work she must do in addition and backstage in relation to her primary student activities:

> *I see it as an extra job I have, because when I am obliged to focus on all the things related to psychiatry, and I have to apply for an extra state education grant,*

> *I need to talk about and use a lot of energy on a lot of hard personal stuff. Which I then again need to spend time and energy to process afterwards.*

As described by Beate and Caroline, this kind of work takes place at multiple levels. As we will return to later, the extra work is both practical and emotional work where feelings of belonging are under pressure. They must demonstrate their legitimacy of belonging at an institutional level in terms of the internal study progression, at a social level for living up to socioculturally created norms, values and beliefs and at an emotional level regarding subjective negotiations of blurry boundaries in demonstrating that they are proper and capable students. The work is practical in the sense that it takes considerable time to repeatedly collect the appropriate documentation, write the applications, and go to doctor's appointments. It is emotional in the sense that it reminds them about prior difficulties, and reactivates traumas of failures or being in a crisis. All in all, many of the different forms of coordinated activities around and in their student life create a space of subjectivity confronting them with norms and ideals of demonstrating the proper belonging and standards which very few students are capable of living up to. However, they are accountable to these ideals to provide an appropriate explanation or documentation in response. To the teacher or supervisor, this form of coordinated extra work is invisible and uncorrelated with their academic work, the institutionalized educational frontstage, leaving it unrecognized as something that requires much skill to navigate and overcome. As institutional ethnographers, we worked towards clarifying how these effects influenced students' life differently, in ways not always obvious to them but as always empirically embedded and linked to practices and institutions elsewhere outside education (Smith, 2005).

When exploring the work students had to do in order to find help and support, what help and support they searched for and why, how they had to plan for weekly doctor's appointments and who they had to coordinate with, it gradually became clear that the extra work had to be understood as both a practical and embodied emotional form of knowledge. By listening, we started to realize that the extra work needed to be understood as a double burden, and that mental illness, diagnoses and being disabled were related to the conceptual power of an educational and occupational ideology in contemporary society. In their talk about how needing extra help and support created feelings of cheating, being left behind, or not being capable enough, they mirrored an authoritative ideology of self-reliance as a defining characteristic of the sense of belonging, not only in education but society in general. Following elusive but distinct and powerful ideas of the withholding of being able, capable and resilient, a student typology formed within an economic order emphasizing employability, entrepreneurialism, competitiveness and flexibility as core qualifications. This form of neoliberal regime of ruling relations[2] has created close connections between education, employability and the economy.

The inspiration from institutional ethnography helped us explore how logics of deficit from the psychiatric diagnostic system, the psychological field and the medical paradigm (Beresford, 2002, 2020; Beresford & Russo, 2016) were playing a part in the systems that the students encountered and how they contained understandings of what a proper and resilient student should look like and be able to do. This was somewhat surprising. Within the Nordic relational model of disability, impairment is recognized, situated and interwoven in a network of relationships between bodies, minds, society, welfare systems and cultural understandings (Goodley, 2018, p. 6). Danish educational legislation states that students with disabilities or functional impairment should be compensated in order to be able to "complete the education in the same way as other students" (SPS Act §1). Nevertheless, in many of the systems, such as special pedagogical support, there is first a process of getting the right documentation, which runs through processes of diagnosing the deficit(s). The logic is that students have a detectable deficit within an unspecific standard of a given normality concerning student participation in education, which the systems should compensate for. In the medical model, mental illness, functional impairments and disabilities are primarily developed from a biopsychological epistemological understanding (Goodley, 2018, p. 3). Hence, instead of changing the conditions for studying, the way to get approved was based on an individualized deficit paradigm where individual deficits were the trigger for drawing the line between help and support and the lack of help and support.

We did not hear of a single case where the knowledge from help and support systems was transferred into changing the learning environment. In that sense it became clear how help and support systems were crucial in providing individual support but often also exposing dire needs for change in the collective learning environment or delivering knowledge that could lead to changes in the overall structural conditions for studying. This implies that rather than challenging the structural conditions or perceptions of what counts or are constructed as normal human interventions towards disability, impairments or mental health issues, it becomes a matter of adjusting, modifying and adapting the individual to contemporary conditions within society (Titchkosky, 2011). The approach is pathogenic in the sense of maintaining an individual model of deficits within a generalizing standard of normality, or as Dan Goodley writes: "And in so doing posits the normal as already there in the background not requiring interrogation nor consideration (as if we already know what normal actually is)" (2018, p. 4). In relation to the field of education, this can be translated to a situation where interventions set the student as their primary object for cure, treatment, change or guidance rather than changing the physical, structural or sociocultural circumstances in the learning environment as an effort towards developing better conditions for participation.

"Then I set aside Wednesday for practical things"

This process of objectification relative to systemic standards was very much the case for Kasper, a student of science. Kasper contracted a brain disease when he was a child. He had to be in a wheelchair for half a year, and still has trouble with walking even short distances. But the disease also affected the part of his brain that coordinates structure and planning in his everyday life. Therefore, Kasper needed extra help planning when to read what, when to apply for extra time for exams, and which courses to take now and which to postpone. But in order to obtain the physical remedies and the professional assistance, and establish a time-space of accessibility for himself as a disabled higher education student, Kasper had to be in constant dialogue with a wide variety of government agencies. They became an important part of Kasper's work of coordinating and organizing a higher education time-space of accessibility. For instance, it took Kasper two years to get a car designed for his disability and approximately the same time to be approved for disability allowance. When moving between the locations for lectures, Kasper struggled with the timetable organized as a standard student physical time-space movement. Initially, he had to demonstrate the required amount of walking of a standard student even though he becomes tired quickly. Trying to overcome the obstacles of being disabled within the standard time-space orchestration gradually led to psychosocial difficulties. His psychosocial state was greatly exacerbated by the subsequent amount of work it required to manage his disability in the many forms of systems with often long and retroactive deadlines. As he explains:

> *Then I set aside Wednesday for practical things . . . to call the council. . . . I have to call them today about my disability allowance (for a state grant), which it has taken me a year and a half to get. . . . There are always some practical things I can do on Wednesdays related to my disability.*

Ultimately, Kasper "walked around with a lot of question marks" to which he struggled to find answers. These were questions about what significance his disability would have for his internship, if and how he could have more time for his exams, where he should apply for extra time and how he could get help to develop a structure in his student life. The questions ran around in his head and prevented him from concentrating on studying. He ended up stopping attending a course to try to create more time in his life and to relieve some of the stress. He was close to dropping out. Kasper had a mentor via "special pedagogical support" who helped him with structure, but he stopped when Kasper was still in his first semester. Kasper was not automatically given another mentor and was without a mentor for three semesters. He almost dropped out because he did not know how, when and where to apply for extra time for exams, and thus did not do the exams. It was not until he contacted a student counsellor directly that he received help and a new mentor.

Within critical disability research, the generalizing and standardized ways of arranging physical and social spaces have to a large degree been understood in Foucauldian terms as biopolitical processes of subjectivation. This means that disability, impairment and mental health issues become a very real reality through the subjective experience of *ability* manifested as being able or disabled (Goodley & Runswick-Cole, 2016). This includes the understanding that the historically changeable discourses about normality influence individuals in the way they perceive themselves as citizens (Goodley, 2018, p. 6). In the field of education, that involves everything from the ability or capability to read, write, discuss or reflect as well as walking, sitting, talking and participating in distinct ways through time and space (Titchkosky, 2011). From the perspective of critical disability studies, power dynamics of subjectification can be seen to influence students' self-understanding as negotiations of properness and shame (Burke, 2017, see also Chapter 5) as it takes place in ongoing constructions of the oppositions between normal and abnormal or able and disabled. The case of Kasper illustrates this point but with the theoretical corrective of him showing the effort and implications of trying to refute the subjectivation taking place, although, as illustrated, it implied carrying an extra workload in being responsible for overcoming barriers and constructing a student life appropriate to a disabled student. As stated by Smith, negotiations and demarcations of the properness/non-properness or able/disabled divide must be explored and understood as real social activities taking place within people's actual coordination of activities in institutional settings. For Kasper, ultimately, the practical work and emotional strain places such a demand on his time and energy that he chooses to study five European Credit Transfer System (ECTS) credits less than the standard time per semester. In a sense, he converts the work activities from a course to the extra work he may undertake to make his student life coherent by explaining his self-responsibility for reconfiguring his conditions for studying. Kasper himself must do the work of organizing and coordinating a course of study that sets boundaries for participation in time and space and where he can become able as a student. The practical dimension of the extra work became an effort to try to rearrange himself around the ideal of an able proper student. This knowledge was embodied in Kasper as "the problem that has no name" (Smith, 2005, p. 78). It became tangible as a set of question marks and evolved into a psychosocial strain regarding the feeling of being misplaced and having to fight to create an educational time-space of belonging mirroring his disability.

"Who is better to talk to than me?"

James is very unlucky – if things can get worse, they will. James and his family spend about one day a week at the doctor's or in hospital. There is always something that needs to be taken care of. Based on his prior experience, James has learned always to plan for the worst possible scenario. That is also why he started to learn rules and reforms to the extent of knowing the wording and loopholes better than student counsellors. James explains how the head of studies cannot stop rolling his eyes and sighing deeply when James approaches. He knows that James has come with a new difficult question that will take a long time to sort out. James is not the standard student and helping or merely accommodating him is definitely time-consuming. But the feeling of hostility and obstacles combined with an episode where James felt a teacher publicly shamed him in class have resulted in James getting anxiety attacks when approaching campus.

As with James, it was a common story that students who did the extra work of finding help or work within the institutional complex of rules, laws and paragraphs to accommodate their studies also became go-to people to trust for other students experiencing difficulties or in need of help. But as James here elaborates, when navigating institutional loopholes, he is constantly reminded of the time and effort he simultaneously must put into being and feeling like an exception to the proper student:

> *There was a time where I read those stupid reforms so thoroughly that I knew all the exceptions. . . . The people I studied with, instead of going to the student counsellors, they came to me in advance, because they knew I had most likely been in one of those shitty situations. So, who is better to talk to than me?*

The knowledge and the status he gained amongst other students as an institutional knower came with the price of a narrative of being on the sidelines as a troubled student. This excerpt illustrates James's difficulty in figuring out the complexity in systems built for those who are an exception to the standardized mass of students. James ends up knowing the intricate details more extensively than the student counsellors. Based on a feeling of frustration at constantly encountering barriers, James had to spend a substantial amount of time to learn who to talk to, what to ask for, when to ask for it, and what rule applies to what circumstance. The wrong advice he was given resulted in him not getting a higher student allowance for several months. That meant a great deal of money for a young man with two children and a wife who suffers from a chronic illness and a family already facing dynamics of social inequality in their life. But he also found alliances within the system. Based on his former experiences, James learned to only talk to one specific counsellor that he could trust would present the correct information and stand up for him. He made sure to always get the advice in writing in case something went wrong, and his counsellor assured him that she would help him if the advice she gave him turned out to be wrong or insufficient. Having to navigate the complex systems in a battle to maintain accessibility clearly affected his understanding of being a proper student and was associated with feelings of resignation, anger and distrust towards the educational system. It was common amongst the interviewed students that the extra work within the systems entangled with their feelings of well-being and could spur difficult subjective introspective negations of their right and place in higher education. This was often referred to as the feeling of a hostile system sending out a signal that they were unwanted, importunate and bothersome. As with James, if the students were lucky to locate a teacher, counsellor or professional that believed in them and fought their case, these individuals were often described as *humans rather than systems* and as counterparts to a hostile system with connections to the institutional framework of accessibility, which the students felt was working to exclude them from the educational community. Being in the space of extra work in that sense produced the feeling of getting lost, overwhelmed and exhausted from moving through administrative labyrinths trying to adhere to the institutional demands. Meeting a professional within the system that set aside the rulings of expulsion in favour of talking and helping at eye level, who believed in them, and helped to boost their self-esteem was often described as the decisive factor for not giving up and dropping out.

". . . do I sound too ill or not ill enough?"

The psychosocial dimension of fighting to stay as a student or finding a way back to a legitimate studying position often developed around a matter of frustration at having to carry the double burden of feeling challenged mentally or physically while also being weighed down by the practical and psychological dimensions of being marked with deficits in comparison to societal norms of properness. One such example comes from Beate. She has broken off with her father and her mother is supported by social security. Her parents cannot support her financially and she is dealing with mental illness to a degree that makes it impossible for her to handle the programme and have an extra job for additional income. It makes her rely on getting both the state education grant and a disability allowance to complete her studies. As a structural condition, political reforms shortened the period students can obtain the state education grant, which greatly affects delayed students like Beate. At the time of the interview, the disability allowance was as mentioned paid out retroactively, which makes her financial situation highly insecure. At the same time, it is very difficult to be granted the disability allowance. Beate explains:

> *[Y]ou need to show, that you retroactively were so ill that you couldn't be a full-time student . . . it's based on such a very delicate balance. And with the extra grant you need to demonstrate in the application that you are able to complete your studies but unable to take on a job in addition to studying. So it's all about, these sentences, you know, I have really been down into minute detail in describing my condition like: does this word make me sound too ill or not ill enough?*

If the application is rejected, she will probably have to drop out without a finished degree and go deeper into debt, pushing her towards an even more socially exposed position. Beate must work at deciphering the inherent system logics that constitute the coordinating link between her written words in the application and the case workers working as representatives of a system built to assess whether her illness disables her to a degree that prevents students like Beate from supporting their state educational grant with an extra job. She must write about her condition and what she cannot do in her everyday life without sounding too ill to even complete a programme. The case workers, on the other hand, must evaluate the application within a logic of economic accountability that does not correlate with a student perspective. Beate elaborates how this work of decoding what the professionals value is like balancing on a knife edge in the descriptions of her illness and even her choice of words. Working at overcoming the selective criteria has made her an expert on her own illness and on finding a delicate description of herself as neither too ill nor too well. Beate's work of describing her deficits and disability is also linked to coordination with other institutional expert systems such as the medical, psychological, and psychiatric paradigm, since she is dependent on having their statements as documentation. This means that Beate repeats her story of being ill to a large number of professionals; she visits new doctors, new psychiatrists and new psychologists again and again. In every encounter Beate must re-represent herself as disabled relative to the norms of ableness and capability of what she cannot do and live up to:

BEATE: *And a lot of it is dependent on your own description when I see new psychiatrists, where I AGAIN have to present my case, and they AGAIN have to write their assessment.*
INTERVIEWER: *By again you mean that you have already told your story elsewhere?*
BEATE: *Yes, and it's exhausting that I simply can't say, look, here is my medical record, try to look at what they wrote during my treatment. Why isn't that enough?*

To be approved for professional state support, psychosocial problems often need to be translated into a standard set of diagnostic categories. A key aspect of the work knowledge acquired by the student doing the extra work is learning to decode and to figure out how to work around these understandings and what the requirements are and how the application will be valued by the support systems. In that process, psychosocial problems transgress mental and bodily states; they become translated into categories that intersect with psychological and psychiatric discourses that change the space of subjectivity, which students like Beate are confronted with and in relation to which they learn to understand their own value and ableness.

"It is the saddest story you can tell about yourself"

The work of repeatedly describing her difficulties has a self-reinforcing effect, creating a problematic echo chamber since it forces her to constantly recall unpleasant episodes of situations where she has been mentally ill or has failed at fulfilling societal and educational norms. This reinforces her doubt of her own capability of being a student:

BEATE: *Where I think about it as an extra job I have. Because when I have to relate to the psychiatry and I have applied for an extra state grant, then I have to talk about and use a lot of energy on a lot of hard stuff, which I spend time to process. I have applied for an extra state grant, and then I started to have very unpleasant dreams about all the stuff I had written about. I've applied for an extra grant for a master's, which I could not complete. And then suddenly, I remembered all my teachers, you know. So I had a lot of dreams about it.*
INTERVIEWER: *It reactivated your bad memories?*

BEATE: *Yes, and that is something that people don't think much about, but that is actually one of the reasons why I didn't apply for an extra state grant last semester. Because it takes up so much of my energy and time and other stuff that I really need to have the mental resources to do it. It is a kind of extra job, and it is the same with the therapy.*

Her extra work is double work. As with the therapy that opens the wounds of her previous traumas, she must process it afterwards. This work takes place in the shadows, being associated and intersected with a structural stigma of mental illness relative to norms of capability. Re-entering traumatic memories is something Beate in one way tries to avoid as part of her recovery process but as a prerequisite for financial and pedagogical support, it becomes her frame of reference for the criteria for adaptability where she fails. Waiting and handling the subsequent emotion becomes work at handling the institutional coordination of being a student working in the support systems framed by strong deficit logics (Smith, 2005). As she states, the way documentation is constructed simultaneously constructs a subjective space that highlights the aspects of her life that do not fit the category of a regular or proper student. The elements created for supporting students in some of the systems also remind them of their incapability (Goodley, 2018, p. 4). To Beate, this involves the subjective work of dealing with thoughts and emotions produced by the deficit framework:

> *I have several days when I'm writing it [state disability grant] where I simply can't do anything, I mean university work. Because it . . . you get so demotivated. I really get so demotivated by it. You know, I almost feel like, well, have I even got what it takes to be a student? It just sounds so. It is the just saddest story you can tell about yourself.*

As Beate states, her situation of requiring extra help means that she has to represent herself in the saddest non-able version of herself, thus overshadowing all her competencies and qualities as a human being and an academic.

Maintaining a foothold in higher education

It was remarkable and overwhelming to witness the effort and self-responsibility mobilized by the students in their insistence on maintaining a foothold as active students. It was primarily a battle they had to fight on their own, overcoming systemic and structural obstacles that severely challenged feelings of belonging.

Exploring the actual work of students having to make an extra effort to achieve educational conditions that could accommodate them as students helped us to uncover the complexity for students placed or trapped in between two institutional regimes in relation to higher education culture and practices. Being a student with a disability, illness or functional impairment, or having developed psychosocial problems relative to higher education discourses and cultures implied navigating in quite different and contradictory sets of systems, codes, norms, laws and rules that often became an excluding force. Recovering was time and energy consuming work often accompanied by a separate timetable for visits to the doctor, psychologist, psychiatrist, mentors and study counsellors, and coordinating with administrative staff or the local council. All this extra work was not perceived by the students as recognized and acknowledged within the educational or occupational system of ruling as work relevant to their studies. Instead, it led to feelings of being trapped between the need for taking the time and spending the energy on recovering and the fear of being left further behind in the competitive race for relevant employable skills in comparison to fellow students.

It became visible how the students had to navigate a bifurcated reality divided by a set of hierarchic values. Working on recovering was accompanied by feelings of being misplaced and unworthy as a student in higher education and framed in contrast to values of the self-reliant and independent student. However, it required immense work, resources and skills to find, activate and use different forms of support, therapy and help. The primary work of being a student understood as doing assignments, going to lectures, and having a relevant part-time job constituted the frontstage of higher education with the extra work of obtaining and reclaiming a space for belonging as the backstage activities often associated with stigma and decoded by the students as low status activities best to be hidden as a strategy to avoid radiating weakness (Goffman, 1959).

Much of the extra work was caused by the framework surrounding students that failed to accommodate those who did not fit the temporal and economic standard of the contemporary ideal typological student. The students had also learned to understand their difficulties as individual deficits, as a lack of resilience and something to find personal adjustments for, whether through changing their physical and psychological dispositions or the temporal, cultural or financial conditions for studying. Students' extra work unfolded as coordinated practices with different professionals and systems to answer the question of how to demonstrate the contextual and situated criteria for belonging. It was often, as illustrated, burdensome practical and emotional work, which thus created a problematic understanding of how a proper student acts, talks, walks, lives, achieves and performs. Help and support systems, although they indisputably provided important help at critical points in the students' lives, were in that sense also caught up in the same logic of trying to normalize students to participate in an unproblematic framework of what a normal student is or should be, i.e. one which maintains and reproduces the imaginary student. To a large degree, conditions for studying in higher education and many of the state-initiated support systems were ruled by logics of financial accountability and deficits rather than working explicitly with a student perspective in which students trying to overcome difficult periods in their life wish to be seen and understood as competent students and recognized for being prospective academics.

Notes

1 Here Smith makes a reference to Betty Freidan's first chapter of *The Feminine Mystique* from 1963.
2 Dorothy Smith conceptualizes ruling relations as "that extraordinary yet ordinary complex of relations that are textually mediated, that connects us across space and time and organize our everyday lives – the corporations, government bureaucracies, academic and professional discourses, mass media, and the complex of relations that interconnect them" (Smith, 2005, p. 10). For Smith, it was important to discuss the problem of how women did not appear as agents or subjects within the ruling relations in the late twentieth century but were instead subordinated by a gendered organization and division of everyday life activities and experiences.

References

Beresford, P. (2002). Thinking about 'mental health': Towards a social model. *Journal of Mental Health, 11*(6), 581–584.

Beresford, P. (2020). 'Mad': Mad studies and advancing inclusive resistance. *Disability & Society, 35*(8), 1337–1342. https://doi.org/10.1080/09687599.2019.1692168

Beresford, P., & Russo, J. (2016). Supporting the sustainability of mad studies and preventing its co-option. *Disability & Society, 31*(2), 270–274. https://doi.org/10.1080/09687599.2016.1145380

Burke, P. J. (2017). Difference in higher education pedagogies: Gender, emotion and shame. *Gender and Education, 29*(4), 430–444. https://doi.org/10.1080/09540253.2017.1308471

Burke, P. J., & Crozier, G. (2014). Higher education pedagogies: Gendered transformations, mis/recognition and emotion. *Journal of Research in Gender Studies, 4*(2), 52–67. ISSN: 2164–0262.

Davies, B. (2000). *A body of writing 1990–1999*. Alta Mira Press.

Goffman, E. (1959). *The presentation of self in everyday life*. University of Edinburgh.

Goodley, D. (2018). Understanding disability: Biopsychology, biopolitics, and an in-between-all politics. *Adapted Physical Activity Quarterly, 35*(3), 308–319. ISSN 0736-5829.

Goodley, D., & Runswick-Cole, K. (2016). Becoming dishuman: Thinking about the human through dis/ability. *Discourse: Studies in the Cultural Politics of Education, 37*(1), 1–15. https://doi.org/10.1080/01596306.2014.930021

Hannam-Swain, S. (2018). The additional labour of a disabled PhD student. *Disability & Society, 33*(1), 138–142. https://doi.org/10.1080/09687599.2017.1375698

Smith, D. E. (2005). *Institutional ethnography: A sociology for people*. AltaMira Press.

SPS Act §1. (2021). https://www.retsinformation.dk/eli/lta/2020/69

Titchkosky, T. (2011). The *question of access: Disability, space, meaning* (2nd ed.). University of Toronto Press.

9 From battling to belonging in higher education

In this final chapter, we recapitulate our most important analytical points and findings about students' perspectives on their experiences of psychosocial problems and their associated battles for belonging and recognition in higher education. Throughout the book's analyses, we have seen that unfolding psychosocial problems as subjective experience often entails intersections of different challenges and struggles. Some relate to biographical experience and others are a result of more recent events. It is important to emphasize that during our exploration of students' experiences of belonging and recognition, we have listened to both moments of despair and testimonies of empowerment. What we learned from taking the student perspective on psychosocial problems in that sense corresponds with broader issues: students' subjective experiences of managing psychosocial problems mirror complex processes of establishing a sustainable student life and a position within educational, social, cultural and institutional contexts.

We can conceptually rephrase the emotional processes of distress and understand them as work (Smith, 2005) constitutive of identity, membership of communities and participation in social practices. From the students, we learn about the resources that they possess and have to mobilize in order to mitigate the powerful mechanism or dynamics of social selection and institutional selection (Jørgensen, 2018). Shame, mental distress and feelings of exclusion from communities in higher education are the equivalent of students fighting against social power dynamics of exclusion. From a subjective standpoint, these situations often reactivate prior life-historical experiences of marginalization, abandonment, harassment or exclusion that influence their self-understanding as 'proper' or 'not proper' in an academic context. Students' feelings of belonging and recognition become a matter of identity unfolding relative to values attached to the idea of becoming a graduate.

Five themes are recurrent. Firstly, students *constantly negotiate* their position or identity as students – processing, understanding and evaluating their ups and downs, thoughts and actions in relation and comparison to (imagined) other students, institutional structures and societal values. Secondly, students often turn the battling against themselves with the emotion of *shame* as a psychosocial response to processes of exclusion and marginalization. Thirdly, students struggle against *time* when falling behind the institutionalized progress and speed

DOI: 10.4324/9781003221029-9

requirements with the consequence of becoming an asynchronous student, a position associated with stigma of not fulfilling societal norms for a creditable temporality. Fourthly, students in multiple ways and contexts *struggle to become acknowledged members* of the social communities in their higher education institutions. Finally, when psychosocial problems arise, students often *struggle to get help*, to locate and gain access to appropriate support systems, varying between basic student counselling, consultations with doctors and actual psychological or psychiatric diagnosis and treatment. All these efforts represent different kinds of identity work students with psychosocial problems have to do and deal with, as described in Chapters 4–8. Reformulating them as work (Smith, 2005), this chapter approaches students' battles for belonging and recognition with a focus on the resources they possess and activate while negotiating their identities as proper students and as worthy members of society. Additionally, we focus on the knowledge provided by the students' experiences as a learning and developmental potential for higher education.

With our poetic representations, we provided an analysis of how students negotiate self-understandings in relation to different social and institutional settings, constantly moving back and forth between 'looking at themselves' from the inside and from their (imagined) outside (cf. Chapter 4). By formulating this particular analysis in the format of poetic representations (Görlich, 2016; Wulf-Andersen, 2012), we wanted to disturb the dominant scientific voice of academic genre conventions and of us as researchers and, in a form and language close to the reflection processes of students, emphasize the sensory and emotional work students with psychosocial problems are doing to negotiate their identities. In this way, we aimed to begin our analyses by showing rather than explaining the complexity of the many intersecting orientations in students' reflections on themselves as students and how students (e)valuate themselves in the light of cultural and societal discourses and norms concerning higher education and psychosocial problems.

The intense societal focus on the importance of education as a vehicle of identity formation sets the scene for feelings of being inadequate compared with other students if one cannot complete education 'like everyone else can' (cf. Chapter 5). It is associated with shame to represent oneself as someone who cannot meet the criteria for fulfilling contemporary study conditions. In discussing shame, with the examples of Alicia, Molly and Signe, we analysed how shame relates to different aspects of higher education: to finding a place and sense of belonging, to working and writing practices and to dilemmas of getting support. We demonstrated how cultural and institutional interpretations and 'narratives of the good student' constitute some students as the opposite, that is, non-standard or not proper students, and how negotiating a position as a good student is hard work. This concurs with research that has pointed out the subtle marginalization of students with diverging conditions for and forms of participation, such as part-time students, within the institutionalized understanding of what the prototype of how the privileged, 'typical,' 'authentic' or 'regular' student figure looks and acts (Thomas, 2019), namely as a young, full-time, in time and self-propelled student (Gravett & Ajjawi, 2021, p. 3). In our case, the result was that many of the students attempted to change themselves by using psychologists or by doing mindfulness or exercise as an effort to bolster their physical and mental stamina as a reaction to the pressure they felt. In addition to changing themselves mentally and physically, they would work on their daily routines and the places and networks they were associated with to make everything look 'right.' The result was sometimes that they felt uncomfortable or not really present and had a guilty conscience for feeling that way. It was also obvious for us that these strategies were primarily individual responses to institutional and structural conditions, transforming external pressure into a question of being resilient and robust enough. Lack of belonging, often perceived as shameful and taboo, is only sparsely addressed in educational contexts, is often said to be caused by previous life-historical experiences and is frequently turned inward into self-criticisms of personal qualities, qualifications and the right to belong. Thus, an important focal point is the hard work it takes to live up to institutional norms, values and settings and silenced battles of shame for students who feel unable to do that work.

We have shown how temporal institutional structures in higher education lead to continuous battles against time and contribute to student inequality. The implications of not having time enough, of not being able 'to set the pace' by oneself and of the imperative of completing one's education as fast as possible were highlighted in the analyses of the cases of Jannie, Esther and Nanna, identifying the identity work associated with time and the capability of managing everyday time structures (cf. Chapter 6). In recent decades, there has been a remarkable change in the temporal logics and timescapes (Adam, 1998) of higher education. This has mostly been a consequence of economic governance in the modernization of the public sector and state institutions, turning educational institutions towards the global knowledge race (see Chapter 2). However, ideas of teaching quality and academic capability also intertwine with temporal structures in, for example, the translation of a standardized educational planning model with a specific amount of work attached to the achievement of each ETCS point and of the complete education. Furthermore, several national reforms have implemented time, structure and effectiveness as a push factor for continued enrolment, which consequently acts as a new form of management or governance. We argued that this creates significant sorting dynamics linked to time structures and asynchrony, where particularly European Credit Transfer System (ECTS) time and a tendency to highlight tempo over learning challenge the sense of belonging for students participating in higher education at a slower pace. As stated by the students, the individual robustness required to keep up with the institutional timescape is paramount, and time structures sometimes counteract efforts to hang on to (part-time) education in periods of physical or mental illness.

To 'feel at ease socially' or to feel safe is a fundamental precondition to focus on the academic part of participation in higher education. Here, we have pointed out another kind of work students have to do to become members of academic and social communities within and outside higher education. It is a vulnerable position to be on the periphery of the student community; however, based on our analyses, we concluded that joining or establishing communities is considered students' own business and responsibility (cf. Chapter 7). Both Louise and William experienced exclusion from student communities, and they both, individually and independently, had to find relevant, sustainable ways forward. Their interest in their subjects played an important role in driving their identity development, and their respective biographies reflect strongly in the actions they take. Rather than being alone, they both become active by joining new communities. Through their own agency, they both manage to turn their situation around, by finding compensatory communities and by creating inclusive learning communities. Communities providing positive recognition, even if related to their academic interests, are not so readily provided or facilitated by educational institutions.

Our analyses have pointed out the 'extra job,' the enormous amount of (paper) work students with psychosocial problems have to do to receive formal recognition of legitimate problems, as a precondition to get help and support or an extension of their studies. This work to document their ill-being repeatedly forced students to tell 'the saddest story' of themselves. Obtaining extra help, waivers, advice, extra time, aids, etc. had already put the students in a deviating position relative to the standardized normal criteria, which are symbolically expressed by the figure of the proper student. The students are by no means passive actors in this process. They develop a wide range of strategies to maintain a foothold within higher education, and they work intensely to find appropriate help, support or treatment (cf. Chapter 8). From the stories of Caroline, Beate and Kasper, we saw how students' self-documentation work is necessary and crucial to keep a foothold in education. Further, we argued that the students do an enormous amount of extra work of self-modulation, the work to change (understandings of) themselves through therapy, or of culture building, the work to challenge and change institutional and social conditions for belonging. This is often invisible work.

Across these five thematic analyses, by drawing on the concept of 'work' (Smith, 2005), we wish to illustrate how hard the students are working to achieve belonging and recognition in different kinds of communities, such as families, friends, higher education and society as a whole. It clearly emerges from our analyses that students feel they need to transform or alter themselves and their identity. The development of an academic identity, be that a positive or negative experience, always involves a negotiation of belonging that can change depending on what happens in a student's life. This is part of the learning process involved in coming to understand oneself in a new light and developing a subject position as a good student, a competent academic and a contributing member of society. However, the extent to which these students' battles take shape as individual struggling is striking. Across all the cases, it is evident that individualization is institutionalized in higher education teaching and learning. It revolves around the idea of proper or good students as independent and capable of coping with difficulties by themselves. They have to prove their legitimacy on their own, and the structural and institutional conditions for participation and legitimacy are based on and oriented towards deficits and shortcomings of individuals.

Accordingly, the general picture is that help and support reside in disembedded systems based in the field of special pedagogy. Problems are formulated as individual students' problems and are to be handled by professional counsellors, psychologists and therapists outside the primary learning environments. These professionals are unquestionably doing an excellent job[1] and the students typically appreciate the help and support they receive from them. Nevertheless, this is an example of how institutional patterns of (mis)recognition end up as individual problems, which students have to handle on their own. This implies the different kinds of work mentioned earlier and the resources the students are able to mobilize to stay in higher education.

Learning from the student perspective

The relationship between the subjective, institutional and societal levels has been central in our analysis, and by using the term *psychosocial problems,* we emphasize the double perspective of nuancing and deepening our understanding of student experiences while also reflecting on how they are being represented. Examining student experiences in an institutional perspective inspired by ethnography and biography (Smith, 2005), we emphasize and appreciate all the work students are doing and their many resources. We have shown how the predominant representation of psychosocial problems on an individual level is complicit in a situation where students experiencing problems have to battle continuously to achieve a sense of belonging and recognition in higher education. We have also stated that approaching the above-mentioned double perspective of the problem from a student perspective can both generate new knowledge and shed light on new nuances of students' psychosocial problems and contribute to new forms of representation and hopefully new ways to enhance student well-being.

The poetic representations are an important contribution to these new forms of representation in providing multiple perspectives to be presented at the same time. Poetic representations do not remove or change the classic methodological issue that representing (marginalized) persons or groups involves the risk of reproducing existing representational problems. Of course, this is also a relevant question when taking a student perspective. We cannot place ourselves beyond this, but by contributing analyses based on a student standpoint, we can show how psychosocial problems are understood, represented and discussed, and how students seem "obliged to think in certain ways" (Somers in McLeod & Wright, 2015, p. 5). By exploring (policy) assumptions behind problems and problem representations, we can enable a discussion of how we can understand and address students' psychosocial problems differently (p. 6).

Importantly, however, taking the student perspective is not an attempt to imply a necessary opposition between students and staff, as the structural conditions in neoliberal higher education in some ways are the same for students and staff (cf. Chapter 2). From the students' experiences, we have realized how staff do not always seem to be able to act appropriately to students indicating ill-being and need of help. Furthermore, we have learned more about how higher education structures and services, including our own institution and its teaching, also seem to have much to learn. It has become even more obvious how certain overall values and financial aspects dominate the educational system and influence staff as well as students. For example, lack of time and academic elitist thinking strongly based on different disciplines influence career systems, which take staff in another direction than spending enough time teaching and supporting the development of academic and social communities. Here, our increased attention to the figure of the proper student or academic, the temporal structures and the patterns of recognition and misrecognition are important issues.

Another contribution is related to our way of emergent listening (see Chapter 3) where we have listened to the students' complex learning processes as *"situated, relational and processual"* aspects of their student life (Gravett & Ajjawi, 2021). We have explored the students' lived, felt and sensed experiences of what available positions they identify for being, becoming and belonging in contemporary higher education. This involved exploring the intersection of institutional power relations and their effect on the conditions for subjectivity under current forms of governmentality based on neoliberal rationalities (Dean, 2015). An example here is when we took the students' standpoint on how their psychosocial problems mismatched their decoding of the ideal student figure, we found out they express this figure as a type of superhuman that never falls ill and never experiences traumas or mental illness. This figure is probably not what higher education means to imply, but in our approach and daily practice, we may imply it anyway.

Furthermore, our study included listening and contextual readings to ascertain what a proper student's identity, body and behaviour ought (not) to be (Burke & Crozier, 2014). It also included listening for the lived responses to the negotiation of idealized forms of subjectivity that take shape as narratives and institutional ruling relations in students' situated everyday life (Smith, 2005). In that sense, battling for belonging has been analysed as students' active process of becoming involved in higher education as a testing of, trying to adhere to and at the same time countering dominant ideals of what is contained in the readings of properness and the ways to become a legitimate member of educational communities and society alike. We have thereby related students' subjective experiences to changes in power relations as they became visible in the drawing of boundaries for belonging as processes of positioning and negotiation of social, cultural, institutional and societal forms of becoming in the intersection with the space of education (Yuval-Davis, 2006). In addition, our insistence on and openness to the unfolding of students' perspectives has worked as an analytical gaze into exploring the processes of learning as part of the testing and shaping of academic and vocational identities. This involves attention to how a biographical trajectory interweaves with experiences of being a participant in educational matters as a material, social and cultural form of practice that defines conditions for belonging and participation. It is a negotiation of identity, which takes place in relation to a conception of a future life and a longing for a recognized place in primary relations, institutions and society (Fraser, 2001; Honneth, 1996).

Belonging and recognition in contemporary higher education

With the neoliberal orientation towards individualism, performance and employability, the question of diverse students' belonging in higher education has become even more relevant and intrusive. During our research on students' experiences of belonging and recognition, it has become evident that the demarcation and boundary for the right to a sense of belonging in higher education today includes much more than strict academic competencies. The contradictory reality the students describe unfolds recognizably within differentiated forms of policy that surround higher education institutions. These have involved a long and gruelling austerity policy that has put educational institutions under financial pressure and under political pressure to become excellent institutions that compete for attracting the best students. At the same time, they need to adhere to a historical shift towards educating more and diverse groups of students. Related to this is a policy concern regarding the promotion and implementation of widening participation as a value-based signal through the inclusion, equality and support of a differentiated student body (cf. Chapter 2, Wilkins & Burke, 2015).

When trying to understand the effects of a neoliberal regime and its implications for educational cultures and institutional ruling relations, it is important to make visible the 'othering' processes that take place. For example, the representations of idealized student figures illuminate the ongoing boundary work of belonging as a differentiated institutional, cultural and pedagogical practice. Such processes of 'othering' are negotiated, articulated and regulated with subsequent consequences for the feeling of belonging. Furthermore, they reveal how recognition is distributed in ways that disadvantage some students because of institutional regimes, implicit academic codes and their associated symbolic meaning. In our study, shame, rejection and the absence of belonging and recognition lead to increased psychosocial problems and identity crises/loss of identity and self-doubt. In particular, feelings of shame are a consistent element across the stories although they can relate to different triggers and norms. Such feelings are well known amongst students from under-represented backgrounds related to institutional processes of misrecognition where, in academic contexts, students are often required to demonstrate a particular set of characteristics, dispositions and attributes (Burke & Crozier, 2014, p. 55). Seen from the students' perspective, shame is in that sense the negation of the ability to demonstrate the correct way of writing, reading and speaking the language of academic culture. Furthermore, students have to create the 'right spare time,' go to student bars, do voluntary work, take on jobs, etc., that is, activities that also contribute to or diminish an academic identity. It implies the mastering of more than mimicking the correct academic behaviour. It also involves mastering a wider set of competencies into what Bernstein (2001) has called weak pedagogical framing of the educational curriculum. He also points out that this is not a question of individual students' deficits, but a question of the institutional reward and recognition principles. This suggests not only helping students with decoding structures, demands, etc. but importantly also developing institutional cultures that are more inclusive.

Furthermore, a neoliberal tightening of the connections between education and employment intensifies what counts as legitimate positions for students experiencing meaningful identifications in relation to educational and societal norms for recognition. Within the rationality of individual accountability, we have noted a distinct internalization of an employability discourse. The students often try to take preventive measures to minimize the probability of ending up in long-term unemployment after graduation. Almost all students have paid work to optimize their CV and of course also to earn money to pay the rent, etc. In that sense, they are very aware of the reciprocal link between societal recognition and being in employment as the main contributory factor to becoming a respectable citizen. The movement in and out of marginalized positions and management of the inherent risk of dropping out is subjectively described as also associated with the risk of becoming unemployed despite a good academic performance, thereby underlining how good marks count as a necessary but insufficient condition in the overall competition.

At the bottom line, all the five themes of this book and the issues and questions included show how the students' identity work also consists of processes of longing for belonging which may reflect institutional and societal centrifugal processes of misrecognition and exclusion. When students with psychosocial problems fight battles in higher education, for example against feelings of unworthiness and shame, this raises questions about inequality. We have argued that mental health and students' psychosocial constitution have become a new sorting mechanism in higher education, intersecting with classic categories such as class, gender and ethnicity (cf. Wulf-Andersen & Larsen, 2020). Our research project has not focused per se on replicating the familiar consensus that higher education works as a socio-economic sorting machine in the society, but our starting point is that this is still a forceful segregating mechanism in effect around the world (Bourdieu, 1998; Domina et al., 2017). In this way, we draw on and supplement classical educational sociology by showing the additional sorting mechanisms for students with psychosocial problems. Bringing forth students' perspectives on experiencing psychosocial difficulties while in higher education has also shed light on the complex and differentiated processes involved in struggling to maintain a position in higher education and the wide range of reasons behind this. This involves understanding and acknowledging the complex ways students' life situations and institutional belonging come to matter in an interconnected wickerwork of everyday life. This has especially been visible in the ways that students for different reasons struggle to maintain their position as legitimate participants, not only as academics. Marginalization and sorting processes take place due to the social, physical, mental, temporal, economic and institutional forms of exclusion. Students long for but find it difficult to maintain a position as legitimate participants when several centrifugal forces are involved.

Reinforcing students' perspectives in collaborative learning approaches

As mentioned in Chapter 1, different kinds of literature on teaching and learning in higher education raise the exemplary question of how different students can feel recognized and experience a sense of academic involvement and belonging in higher education. One focus in this literature is how to develop more inclusive learning environments. This question seems highly relevant in continuation of the above-listed problems of belonging and recognition of students with psychosocial problems. Considering the premises for constructive and inclusive learning environments and the problems of temporality and timescapes, the solution is not solely to reduce speed but also a question of resonance (Rosa, 2019). This is related to our situatedness in and our relationship with the world, that is, subject matters, human relations and our values regarding the good life. This is also reflected in our empirical data: whenever there is a possibility for students to relate in a meaningful way to the academic content and/or community, it becomes a recovery process for the student. In this light, an important step forward seems to be working to create more inclusive learning environments, with more academic and social communities available for all students.

Following on from that, it is important to explore how collaborative learning communities can play a role for students, especially those with psychosocial challenges. Here, students' work is performed through joint tasks and negotiation of common goals and in a community where mutual dependence, joint (synchronous) task solving and joint context characterize participant relations (Wenger, 1998). In other words, it is a construction based on reciprocity and respect, which, however, can be difficult to handle and which requires teachers and supervisors to be included as clear collaborators and mediators with the students. Through an institutional commitment, experiences of communities of practice (Wenger, 1998) can be created in a 'class,' so that mutual obligation to support each other in the learning process extends beyond a project group-delimited community and includes the entire 'class.' This may take place, for example, through short-term collaboration between the teacher and smaller groups of students on selection and planning of teaching elements, collaboration between smaller groups of students to prepare and give presentations, teaching exercises and the like, where all students are involved with different roles and tasks in collaboration with the teacher. Experiences of being allowed to participate and contribute constructively may strengthen all students' feeling of being able to succeed in higher education. In addition, teacher accessibility may help to clarify learning goals and methods, thus providing more transparency, thereby preventing some of the insecurities that students experience. This is about creating cultures of space and respect for diversity and progression for the individual and for the collective and is inspired by approaches based on resource orientation rather than deficit orientation towards students, acknowledging that higher education often fails to engage a wide range of students' resources in teaching and learning. Some pedagogical approaches aim at creating inclusive study environments while also having a critical eye for the power dynamics embedded in teaching and learning scenarios. Approaches such as 'students as partners' (e.g. Cook-Sather et al., 2018, 2017) and co-creative teaching and learning processes (e.g. Bovill et al., 2016; Jensen & Krogh, 2017) are good examples of this, as are joint (research) projects for students and staff (Wulf-Andersen et al., 2015). Such approaches offer a counter-figure to the neoliberal figure of the student as a 'consumer' (Cook-Sather & Felten, 2017; Healey et al., 2014; Matthews et al., 2018) and consider learning situations as mutual and beneficial for both staff and students (Matthews, 2017). Consequently, this type of inclusive learning community presupposes insight, interest, openness and willingness from the teacher and the institution to use innovative forms of teaching. This means new roles for both teacher and students and may therefore also present (additional) challenges to the academic staff. Collaborative initiatives may bring teachers closer to students and meet a number of students' wishes regarding the development of innovative teaching in higher education (Iversen et al., 2016). An inclusive study environment around teaching activities, supported through various elements of co-creative processes (Bovill et al., 2016; Jensen & Krogh, 2017) may have an contagious effect on the value of learning communities that respect diversity by building a climate of trust and encouraging risk-taking (Kilpatrick et al., 2003).

Coming from universities with a long tradition of using problem-based learning and problem-oriented project learning, we know from experience that collaborative learning scenarios create student motivation and engagement and can lead to deep learning of academic disciplines and development of communicative and social skills. We also know that the learning processes involved are complex and challenging and that power struggles may take place within groups (Jensen & Lund, 2016). Consequently, requirements for an inclusive learning community to be feasible are openness, acceptance and understanding of group dynamics, the complex and daunting processes involved and what this means in relation to the psychosocial problems students may experience. Collaborative learning communities thus represent opportunities *if mediated* and supported by teachers/ supervisors but may also create a number of challenges for students with psychosocial problems, especially if they are left alone or excluded, as seen in our data and the analyses in the previous chapters. As we have seen, there is a challenge in working individually in a collaborative learning community, if an institutional commitment does not support it, represented by teachers' interest, care and support for students in general and specifically for those with psychosocial problems. Institutional commitment is essential for collaborative learning communities to succeed and this means continued engagement and responsibility for providing the necessary conditions at all levels of the institution. Institutions must continuously work on creating sustainable pedagogical frameworks and inclusive study environments for students with psychosocial problems in collaborative learning communities. But, there are by no means any universal solutions. Collaborative and co-creative initiatives and study environments may not solve all the problematic issues we have mentioned in this book. Our research has (still) left us with the following critical questions: What basic preventative measures can higher education adopt? Which important policy changes in the processes of structuring and managing are needed? What can work as effective interventions offering better guidance, scaffolding and help for all students and especially those with or at risk of psychosocial problems? Fundamental changes are needed in educational policy, but until that happens improved conditions should, and could, be created for students within the framework of the neoliberal competitive society. Based on our findings, competent facilitation of processes and creation of environments with clear and transparent frameworks for academic work, collaboration and roles are needed to support processes of belonging. Inclusive study environments require transparent and ethically correct group formation processes, as well as an awareness of opening up community opportunities for new students and for students who return their studies after a period of absence. It is essential to be aware of the potentially sensitive aspects, power perspectives and forms of communication of joint learning processes, for example in group work and in feedback situations, and to create routines characterized by inclusivity and recognition. For students, it is also often helpful if a certain degree of flexibility and self-direction/ student direction is possible regarding the focus and organization of students' work. Finally, the need for recognition could be met through structures of acknowledgement that appreciate different students' various contributions focusing on processes and learning over time (hence, formative evaluation) rather than solely summative evaluations of performance.

An analytical model for belonging and recognition

How can higher education institutions be inspired and learn from student experience? What can higher education learn from representing students' problems as psychosocial? Institutions should focus on students' different kinds of work and should emphasize the efforts explicitly and implicitly demanded from and performed by students in order for them to function in higher education, and in order to make higher education function, on an everyday basis. Understanding students' experiences and learning processes as situated and shaped in complex intersections of biographical, institutional and societal dynamics shows how different levels work together in ways that go beyond the individual, such as how institutional norms promote particular strategies and conceptions of self. Also important here are the ways cultural or political currents contribute certain interpretations of what kinds of problems are legitimate or illegitimate for students in higher education to experience, and the formal and informal criteria determining who can pass as a proper or good student. These are inherently institutional issues, concerning institutional responsibility for developing sound learning environments and study programmes based on student diversity, and for the facilitation of belonging and recognition structures and processes embracing diverse students. Making the student experience the centre of attention is in this sense not to promote a focus on individual students. Rather, it implies taking seriously the fact that particular students' complex situations are important prisms through which we can illuminate and discuss a range of belonging and recognition issues in higher education institutions.

We began this book with a quote[2], raising the question of whether higher education knows, maybe even cares, too little about its students' battles. We would like to end the book by bringing student perspectives on students' problems to the foreground in order to understand how different students experience psychosocial problems. We therefore designate this final section as consolidating the contributions of the book in an analytical model. The purpose of the model is to encourage further explorative dialogues and collaborative work with a variety of students and other stakeholders on higher education and student life, including the complex interactions between psychosocial problems and educational contexts and processes.

The analytical model is both theoretically and empirically informed, based on the problems, strengths and suggestions formulated by the students in our research. Its intention is to help any actor in higher education interested in exploring and asking questions of the particular educational context this actor is involved in. The model can be a starting point for insights that refine and nuance our awareness of the conditions higher education institutions and programmes provide for students' belonging. What are the boundaries and where is there room for manoeuvre? How do formal and informal recognition structures sometimes contradict each other? What possibilities are apparent to students? Analysing and becoming more aware of the structures of belonging and recognition in institutions and learning environments is a prerequisite for developing new forms and structures of recognition and belonging, giving due attention to the weak spots, contradictions and pitfalls involved in students' battles for belonging.

This may be represented by the matrix shown in Table 9.1. The horizontal headings are theoretically and empirically inspired by the specific themes dealt with in Chapters 4–8. However, configuring themes in the matrix encourages analytical questions and attention to the ways dynamics of shame, asynchrony,

Table 9.1: Matrix representation of our analytical model.

	Informal recognition	*Formal recognition*	*Temporal structures*	*Structures and facilitation of communities*
Academic subject, content				
Students' social relations, networks				
Physical and virtual space				
Culture, discourse, norms in programme/higher education institution				
Societal circumstances, structures, policy				
Student's biography, personal history				

communities, work and extra work mutually interact and intertwine with processes of belonging and recognition.

An analytical model cannot constitute a direct path to or recipe for more inclusive educational practices. However, it can point out central aspects of students' everyday lives and experiences and assist in the development of an inquisitive exploration of situated student life and belonging processes in higher education settings. Eventually, application of such an exemplary model of systematic explorative dialogue and analysis will be the backbone of the locally situated, collaborative development of study programmes and learning environments with potentials for supporting students' feelings of belonging and recognition.

In the Appendix, we provide a version of the matrix with each box filled in with questions or focal points. This obviously does not represent an exhaustive list, but might spark local work and initiate further development of the matrix, adapted to the specific context.

The model thus prepares for an analytical focus on the work students do, have to do or conceal that they do in order to belong. On the other hand, the model prepares for attention to the work higher education management, staff and counsellors do, do not do or cannot do, to support and promote student belonging.

Working from the analytical matrix, one should always be aware that each box in the matrix we here portray in two dimensions to the student holds a third dimension. All the questions could be asked with respect to not only higher education settings but also all the other contexts and arenas students participate in that surround higher education. When we analyse or discuss for instance students' social relations and networks in higher education settings, we must remember that students are always also 'already involved' in social relations and networks beyond higher education (Neidel & Wulf-Andersen, 2012). This involvement overlaps with or differs from, but always influences, implicitly or explicitly, students' understandings and experience of participating in the social relations and networks of higher education.

This also applies when we ask how students relate to the curriculum and the academic content. This is often relative to and mediated by students' extracurricular interests, engagements and hobbies outside higher education. Access, presence and movements in the university's physical and virtual spaces intertwine with students' movements in other institutional or informal landscapes of residence, treatment or employment. Students' relations to other students and different groups of staff (academic, administrative and counselling staff) and relations to friends, family, boyfriends and girlfriends, therapists, counsellors and employers overlap or mutually affect each other.

The point is that the matrix can assist us in unfolding the profound complexity of belonging processes in higher education. Hopefully, this can make us more aware of how institutionalized patterns of recognition and misrecognition are complicit in students' psychosocial problems and contribute to inclusion and exclusion in higher education.

At a point in history where competing and contradictory discourses interact in complex ways to shape ideas of 'good students' and (il)legitimate problems, a diverse student body struggles to belong in higher education. Learning and identity processes, life if you will, come with barriers, insecurities, frustration, disorientation, anxiety, failure and many other unpleasant surprises alongside the insights, knowledge, realizations, questions, directions and ideas also associated with experience and learning.

Everybody struggles at some point and to some extent on their path through higher education. However, no student should be left alone to think that experiencing or battling with problems is wrong. No student should have to deal with problems, large or small, by themselves. Battles for belonging should be carried into a collective domain to challenge institutional conditions for being a higher education student and definitions of normality in contemporary society. The exploration and discussion of academic and student life problems should be a collective effort across students, staff and management, preferably also including other stakeholders and the political level, in a dialogue with the ambition of including different (student) perspectives, employing different forms of knowledge and resources in the collaborative development of belonging and recognition structures in higher education. A critical reflection based on solidarity of the ways higher education and the people populating it are embedded in sociocultural, political and economic contexts would be an important part of this dialogue. The commitment on this further joint dialogue should continue. Always.

Notes

1. We elaborate on the particular forms of support provided by these professionals in the Danish context in the report "*If they miss one step. . .*" *Counsellors' perspectives on students' well-being problems in higher education* (Stigemo et al., 2021, in Danish).
2. In Chapter 1, we described how the quote "Everyone you meet is fighting a battle you know nothing about. Be kind. Always." was brought to our attention by a student.

References

Adam, B. (1998). *Timescapes of modernity*. Routledge.
Antonsich, M. (2010). Searching for belonging – an analytical framework. *Geography Compass*, 4(6), 644–659.
Bernstein, B. (2001). Pædagogiske koder og deres praksismodaliteter [Pedagogical codes and their modalities of practice]. In L. Chouliaraki & M. Bayer (Eds.), *Basil Bernstein, pædagogik, diskurs og magt* [*Basil Bernstein, pedagogy, discourse and power*] (pp. 69–93). Akademisk Forlag.
Bourdieu, P. (1998). *Practical reason – on the theory of action*. Polity Press.
Bovill, C., Cook-Sather, A., Felten, P., Millard, L., & Moore-Cherry, N. (2016). Addressing potential challenges in co-creating learning and teaching: Overcoming resistance, navigating institutional norms and ensuring inclusivity in student-staff partnerships. *Higher Education*, 71(2), 195–208.
Burke, P. J., & Crozier, G. (2014). Higher education pedagogies: Gendered formations, mis/recognition and emotion. *Journal of Research in Gender Studies*, 4(2), 52–67.

Cook-Sather, A., & Felten, P. (2017). Ethics of academic leadership: Guiding learning and teaching. In F. Wu & M. Wood (Eds.), *Cosmopolitan perspectives on becoming an academic leader in higher education* (pp. 175–191). Bloomsbury Academic.

Cook-Sather, A., Matthews, K. E., Ntem, A., & Leathwick, S. (2018). What we talk about when we talk about students as partners. *International Journal for Students as Partners, 2*(2). https://doi.org/10.15173/ijsap.v2i2.3790

Dean, M. (2015). Neoliberalism, governmentality, ethnography: A response to Michelle Brady. *Foucault Studies, 20,* 356–366.

Domina, T., Penner, A., & Penner, E. (2017). Categorical inequality: Schools as sorting machines. *Annual Review of Sociology, 43,* 311–330.

Fraser, N. (2001). Recognition without ethics? *Theory, Culture & Society, 18*(2–3), 21–42.

Görlich, A. (2016). Afstand, modstand og mestring: Poetiske analyser af unges subjektiveringsprocesser [Distance, resistance and mastery: Poetic analyses of young people's subjectivization processes]. *Psyke & Logos, 37*(1), 225–247.

Gravett, K., & Ajjawi, R. (2021). Belonging as situated practice. *Studies in Higher Education.* https://doi.org/10.1080/03075079.2021.1894118

Healey, M., Flint, A., & Harrington, K. (2014). *Students as partners in learning and teaching in higher education.* Higher Education Academy. https://www.heacademy.ac.uk/system/files/resources/engagement_through_partnership.pdf

Honneth, A. (1996). *The struggle for recognition – the moral grammar of social conflicts.* Polity Press.

Iversen, A. M., Pedersen, A. S., Krogh, L., & Jensen, A. A. (2016). Learning, leading and letting go of control: Learner-led approaches in education. *Sage Open, 5*(4).

Jensen, A. A., & Krogh, L. (2017). Re-thinking curriculum for 21st-century learners: Examining the advantages and disadvantages for adding co-creative aspects to problem-based-learning. In T. Chemi & L. Krogh (Eds.), *Co-creation in higher education: Students and educators preparing creatively and collaboratively to the challenge of the future.* Sense Publishers.

Jensen, A. A., & Lund, B. (2016). Dealing with insecurity in problem oriented learning approaches: The importance of problem formulation. *Journal of Problem Based Learning in Higher Education, 4*(1), 53–70.

Jørgensen, C. H. (2018). Inklusion i erhvervsuddannelse: institutionel selektion og eksklusion i elevfællesskaber [Inclusion in vocational education: Institutional selection and exclusion in student communities]. In S. Baagøe Nielsen, S. Hvid Thingstrup, M. Brodersen, & H. Hersom (Eds.), *Drenges og mænds inklusion på kønnede uddannelser* [*The inclusion of men and boys in gendered education*] (pp. 61–84). Frydenlund Academic.

Kilpatrick, S., Barrett, M., & Jones, T. (2003). *Defining learning communities.* CRLRA Discussion Paper Series ISSN 1440–480X. University of Tasmania.

Matthews, K. E. (2017). Five propositions for genuine students as partners practice. *International Journal for Students as Partners, 1*(2), 1–9. https://dx.doi.org/10.15173/ijsap.v1i2.3315

Matthews, K. E., Dwyer, A., Hine, L., & Turner, J. (2018). Conceptions of students as partners. *Higher Education, 76,* 957–971. https://doi.org/10.1007/s10734-018-0257-y

McLeod, J. & Wright, K. (2015). *Interventing youth wellbeing.* Springer.

Neidel, A., & Wulf-Andersen, T. (2012). The ethics of involvement with the already involved: Action research and power. In L. Phillips, M. Kristiansen, M.

Vehviläinen, & E. Gunnarsson (Eds.), *Knowledge and power in collaborative research: A reflexive approach* (pp. 153–170). Routledge.
Rosa, H. (2019). *Resonance: A sociology of our relationship to the world.* Polity Press.
Smith, D. E. (2005). *Institutional ethnography: A sociology for people.* AltaMira Press.
Stigemo, A., Larsen, L., & Wulf-Andersen, T. (2021). *"If they miss one step. . ." counsellors' perspectives on students' well-being problems in higher education* [In Danish with the title: *"Hvis de først taber ét skridt. . ." Vejledere og rådgiveres perspektiver på mistrivsel blandt studerende i videregående uddannelse*]. Student Life Project, Roskilde University.
Thomas, K. (2019). Rethinking student belonging in higher education: From Bourdieu to borderlands. Routledge/Taylor & Francis.
Wenger, E. (1998). *Communities of practice: Learning, meaning, and identity.* Cambridge University Press.
Wilkins, A., & Burke, P. J. (2015). Widening participation in higher education: The role of professional and social class identities and commitments. *British Journal of Sociology of Education, 36*(3), 434–452. https://doi.org/10.1080/01425692.2013.829742
Wulf-Andersen, T. (2012). Poetic representation: Working with dilemmas of involvement in participative social work research. *European Journal of Social Work, 15*(4), 563–580. https://doi.org/10.1080/13691457.2012.705261
Wulf-Andersen, T., Hjort-Madsen, P., & Mogensen, K. H. (2015). Research learning – how students and researchers learn from collaborative research. In A. S. Andersen & S. B. Heilesen (Eds.), *The Roskilde model: Problem-oriented learning and project work.*
Wulf-Andersen, T. Ø., & Larsen, L. (2020). Students, psychosocial problems and shame in neoliberal higher education. *Journal of Psycho-Social Studies, 13*(3), 303–317.
Yuval-Davis, N. (2006). Belonging and the politics of belonging. *Patterns of Prejudice, 40*(3), 197–214.

Appendix

Appendix

	Informal recognition	Formal recognition	Temporal structures	Structures and facilitation of communities
Academic subject, content	What is recognized or receives recognition – and why (not)? How is recognition expressed? Who are primary or significant 'agents' of recognition?	What is recognized or receives recognition – and why (not)? How is recognition expressed? By whom – who are primary or significant 'agents' of recognition? What kinds of problems are recognized as legitimate (grounds for waivers)?	Flexibility to plan or rearrange the programme (e.g. shift elements of the programme or study part time)? Specific barriers or risks for asynchronous students (e.g. reforms, discontinuation of elements of the programme)?	Pedagogical and didactical organization of study elements? In what ways and to what extent can the organization and working methods enable dialogue with students?
Students' social relations, networks	Which groups and networks are available to students? How do students find or gain access to groups and networks (in class, related to assignments, during breaks, at the student bar)? What do groups and networks contribute (friends, snowballing effect into other networks, access to notes in case of absence)?	Do working methods in the study elements allow or promote students' access to social networks or communities? Is it possible to work in groups? Is it possible to work alone? Which network resources for support are available to students (e.g., teachers, supervisors, academic groups, student counsellors)?	Connection points for students who become asynchronous to maintain or (re)establish social networks? In what ways does the higher education institution or the study programme facilitate students' reconnecting?	What kinds of communities are facilitated by the institution or study programme? What is the variation in formats/content/expected participants? In what ways and by whom (who is responsible, who does the work)? When? (during the course of the programme and students' processes)

158 *Appendix*

	Informal recognition	*Formal recognition*	*Temporal structures*	*Structures and facilitation of communities*
Physical and virtual space	What kinds of spaces are available and accessible for students? Where can students make their mark, their own arrangements? What criteria do students feel they have to meet to use and access these spaces? What is the general culture or practice of use and access?	What kinds of spaces are available and accessible for students? Criteria for use and access?	When are different spaces open for use? What institutional ideas (of e.g. legitimate purpose, working routines, participants, etc.) shape the timescapes and spaces of the institution or programme?	In what spaces is it possible to be part of, find, display or visit student communities? (How) Do different spaces work as connecting points for communities and belonging? Whose communities dominate different spaces (by way of e.g. function, information, arrangements, artwork, online posts, cafeteria)? Where are students, academic staff and student counselling located relative to each other (common spaces or separate)?

Appendix 159

Culture, discourse, norms in programme/ higher education institution	How do higher education management and staff express their expectations and definitions of students (in introductory talks, in feedback, everyday informal communication in class or during breaks)? What are the everyday translations, interpretations and practice of formal rules (bending rules, stigma, preferential treatment)? Relative to whom and what do students compare and negotiate themselves as students?	How do higher education institutions and programmes communicate official expectations and definitions of students (on websites, in presentations and introductory material, etc.)? Formal expectations, demands and assessments of students by higher education and how are these communicated? What are (the key values in) the rules, regulations and frameworks of the visions of the institution – and how are they formulated and communicated? What are formal interpretations and practices for administering rules (precedents, possibility of waiver)? How are they made visible?	How many elements or activities of the programme are students expected to participate in and what workload are they expected to have? Is working at high speed/tempo culturally endorsed and rewarded? What are the possibilities for and consequences of students' adjusting the tempo, setting their own pace?	How are individual and collective working methods and performances referred to, communicated and supported, halted or rewarded? Is individual work and collaboration understood as (associated with) academic competence and excellence? – and how?

	Informal recognition	Formal recognition	Temporal structures	Structures and facilitation of communities
Societal circumstances, structures, policy	How do public debate and the media discursively construct and discuss questions related to students, higher education and academia?	Trends and values underpinning educational policy and reforms? What values, characteristics and specific institutions are prioritized, recognized and valued through the funding structures of higher education? And what does this mean for the quality of education and teaching? Current movements and structures of recognition in the labour market (e.g. conditions of merit, employment and pay)?	Temporal structures and values characterizing the labour market and society surrounding higher education? What are the financial, thus the temporal, conditions for studying (state funding, student jobs, parental financial support)?	How are students, graduates and academics understood and discursively constructed in public and political debate? What performances, contributions and examples are highlighted and praised? What results, qualities, competencies and working methods are emphasized as valuable contributions to society?
Student's biography, personal history	What are the student's prior and current experiences of inclusion or exclusion and (mis)recognition (e.g. bullying, praise, good friends, talents)? What are significant or critical incidents, moments or persons in the student's personal-educational biography (e.g. meeting significant others, turning points)?	What are the student's previous and current experiences of inclusion or exclusion and (mis) recognition (e.g. grades, feedback, being recognized or forgotten by the system) – Consequences?	What characterizes the student's process and timescape (e.g. progress, loops, pauses, lurching)? How does this process or timescape match or mismatch temporal structures of the study programme?	What communities is the student (not) part of? The student's experiences of the establishment and disintegration of communities? Who or what does the student understand as agents in these processes (e.g. herself, other students, staff, institutions, chance)? What needs for facilitation, assistance or support of student communities does the student express?

Index

Note: Page numbers followed by 'n' indicate a note on the corresponding page.

able/disabled divide 133
academics/academic: achievements in higher education, impact of mental illness on 41; and social communities 14, 94, 142, 148; careers 31; learning 91; potential, standard of 85; qualifications, hard work required to obtain 38; success, notion of 108; working life, complexity and unpredictability of 32
acceleration: as 'revelation', analyses of 92; of time 97
acknowledged members, of the social communities 141
administrative procedures, reorganization of 107
Alicia, story of 78–79, 81–84, 89–93, 94
Antonsich, M. 9, 47, 111, 114, 121
asynchronous students 14, 97, 102–105, 107–108, 141

basically feeling secure, sense of 91
being, sense of 128
belonging in higher education: analytical dimensions of 9, 150–153; battling for 8–11, 29–32, 38, 42, 48; complexity of 12; concept of 9–10, 121; in contradictions 29–32; in Danish higher education 48; experiences of 122; 'good students' and recognition structures of 11–12; higher education institutions and programmes 151; impact of communities as a foundation for 110; legitimacy of 130; modes of 10; negotiating and interpreting conditions for 47; place-belongingness 9, 116; politics of 9, 111, 116, 121; process of 47, 116; recognition and 146–147; sense of 9, 12, 47, 78, 110, 130, 142, 146; signifier of 97; status of 126; students' battles for 13, 153; students' feelings of 152; students' sense of identity and 11; and theories of social learning 9; time as a signifier of 107–108
Bennett, A. 97, 101, 105
Bernstein's educational sociology 97, 102
bibliometric research indicator 31
Biggs and Tang's alignment model 5
biography of students 123
biomedical paradigm 3
bipolar disorder 86, 89
bipolarity, notion of 87
Bologna Declaration (1999) 26–28, 100, 105
Burke, P. J. 97, 101, 105

capitalist economy 128
Caroline, story of 125–127, 130, 143
childhood traumas 37
class culture, as imperative for learning 121, 122
classical sociology, of education 96
class universities 31
collaborative (writing) abilities 85
collaborative learning 148–150
collective 'hypocrisy', in higher education 92, 93–94
collective learning 41, 131
Committee for Quality and Relevance in Further Education (Denmark) 23

communicative and social skills, development of 149
communities: academic and social 148; collaborative learning 149; concept of 111, 122; as a foundation for academic work 111–115; journey towards a supportive 118–119; membership, symbols of 91; of practice 10, 148; right for 80; role in renegotiating identity 115–118
completion times, standardization of 29
contract management 23
Council of Europe 26
COVID-19 pandemic 3, 36
creating new opportunities, idea of 26
cultural capital 43, 47

Danish Accreditation Institution 23
Danish educational policy 23–24, 103; focus on public accountability 28; globalization strategy 25; orientations towards internationalization and globalization 24; 'Progress, renewal and development – Strategy for Denmark in the global economy' 25; qualification frameworks 27; reforms in 28–29; on role of universities regarding their societal function 24
Danish Ministry of Higher Education and Science 2, 21, 27
Danish Progress Reform 102
Danish University Act (2003) 24, 32, 103
Davies, Bronwyn 39, 44
deep learning, of academic disciplines 149
Delors, Jaques 24
democratizing education, trajectory of 22
Denmark: educational legislation in 32, 131; national reform policy 26
Denmark, higher education in 6, 13; battling for belonging in 48; democratic influence in 23; European and national policies, influence of 20; global competition in 26; governance of 22; management and education practices in 27; from national autonomy to transnational governance 23–26; neoliberal market-friendly economic policies 24, 30; OECD, role of 24; psychosocial problems 20; public good 21; in welfare state context 20
descending (downward) listening 39

desynchronization, process of 107
disabilities 4
disability allowance 128, 132, 135
distribution of power, between researcher and informant 38
drop-out rates, in higher education 6

economic accountability, logic of 135
education/educational: considerations, notion of 31; cultures 12, 14, 42, 79, 80, 146; institution, role in international competition 24; legislation, in Denmark 32; policy engineering, of higher education 21; qualifications, assessment of 29; research and policy 4; sociology 30, 97, 102, 147; system functions 96
education, rights to: classical sociology of 96; of people with disabilities 4
egalitarian ideals, of education 30
emergent listening, principle of 13, 39, 44, 127
emotion/emotional: acceptance 114; affiliation 11
empirical grounding, notion of 129–131
empirical methods, in analysis of psychosocial problems: interviews 43–46; mapping connections (second interview) 45; metaphors as meta-perspectives (third interview) 45–46; typical week (first interview) 43–45; visit at a chosen location 46–47
employability 32, 37
engagement, process of 10
engineering education 22
English higher education institutions 80
equality: and dynamics of exclusion, ideals of 31; and economy, discourses on 22–23
Esther, story of 96–99, 101, 104, 106–107, 142
eternal student 103–104
EU education policy 27; harmonization of 26; implementation process 28; and national globalization strategy 29; OECD, influence of 29; on quality of higher education 28
European Commission 23–24
European Credit Transfer System (ECTS) credits 14, 27, 28, 97, 100–102, 106, 133, 142
European educational institutions 26
European Higher Education Area (ESG) 28, 33, 33n2

Index

fantasy 10
feeling wrong, notion of 81–84, 89
fighting to stay as a student, psychosocial dimension of 135–136
formal support, dilemmas of getting 86–89
Fraser, Nancy 12
free market, for education 26
Freire, Paulo 37
functional impairments 4, 127–128, 131, 137

gathering skills and competencies, importance of 26
global elitist orientations, relation with local situated needs 31
global knowledge economy 25, 29–30
global universities 31
Goodley, Dan 131
'good student' in higher education 14; dimensions and ideas of 93; emotional experience of 79; expectations and images of 78; images of 92; narrative of 93–94; normative ideas of 78; and recognition structures of belonging in higher education 11–12; synchronized 107; values of 79
grade bonus systems, standardization of 29
'Growth, Competitiveness, Employment' white paper 24

Hannam-Swain, Stephanie 127
higher education: contribution to the development of local communities 31; development of learning environments in 2, 5; discourse about 29; equal access to 22; European policies on quality of 28; individualizing aspects of 123; institutions 4, 21, 23, 151; maintaining a foothold in 137–138; mental health issues 2; pedagogical cultures 30; psychosocial problems in 1, 2–8; public funding of 12; regulation of 21; research-based 21; role in the changes to society 20; shame and becoming in 79–81; social communities related to 8; in social reproduction of economic, cultural and social capital 21; sorting mechanism in 6; structural reforms in 44; students' transitions from high school to 5; *see also* Denmark, higher education in; university education
Honneth, Axel 12, 102, 115, 119, 121
human, as agentic individual 10
human capital theory 22–23
human knowledge 25

identity: development 111, 118, 122–123, 143; formation 10, 47, 118, 122, 127, 141
imagined community 118
immersion, ideals of 32
imposter syndrome 120
individual(ized) work routines, struggling with 84–86
inequality, production of 37
institutional ethnography 15, 51, 127, 130
institutionalized power of ideology 39
institutional selection, dynamics of 140
international cooperation, development of 24
interpersonal skills 115
interviews with students 43–46; bottom-up perspective 43; ethnographic 43; mapping connections (second interview) 45; metaphors as meta-perspectives (third interview) 45–46; typical week (first interview) 43–45

James, story of 133–135
Jannie, story of 96–97, 100, 102
jigsaw metaphor 97–99
jobs, global competition for 32

Kasper, story of 131–133, 143
knowledge: creation, institution for 24; production 29; society, discourse of 23

labour market, of higher education 21, 23–24, 32, 98
Langer, Susanne 51
Law School, decoding of 81–84, 93
learning: as becoming 80; class culture as imperative for 121–122; in communities of practice 111; problem-based 149; social theory of 111; from the student perspective 144–146
life experiences, when encountering today's educational system 39

lifelong learning 25, 32; concept of 24; discourses about 26, 37; policy framework about 26; promotion of 24, 30
life tempo, acceleration of 98
Lisbon, Treaty of 25–26
listening: descending (downward) 39; emergent 13, 39, 44; methodological practice of 39; to students' voices 41
lived time 103, 105–106
loneliness, sense of 113–114, 119, 122
Louise, story of 111–118, 123

Madsen, S. R. 100
managed professionals 28
management reforms, implementation of 20
marginalization of students 141
mass media 38
master's programme, in social science 98
Member States of EU, lifelong learning for growth of 24
mental disorders 2
mental distress 140
mental health problems 114; amongst students in higher education 1; university mental health crisis 3
mental illness 4, 37, 85–86, 98, 129, 131, 142; causes and connotations of 40; experience in relation to everyday practices 7; relation with academic achievements in higher education 41; stigmas and deficit thinking associated with 41
metaphors, as meta-perspectives 45–46
methodological framework, in analysis of psychosocial problems: analysing using a student perspective 47–48; empirical methods 43–46; longitudinal design of 40–43; principle of 38–39; research design 41
misrecognition: politics of 81; symptom of 14
modern welfare state, development of 20
Molly, story of 78, 84–89, 93–94, 141
mutual engagement, development of 10, 121

Nanna, story of 96–97, 101, 103–106, 142
national economy 24
negative social legacy 96
Negt, Oskar 8

neoliberal managerial discourse 20
new public management, implementation of 13, 22–23, 31
Nordic welfares: relational model of disability 131; welfare models 30

objectification, process of 131
obsessive-compulsive disorder 98
occupational worthiness, idea of 80
Okanagan Charter 4

patriarchal sociology, limitations of 51
pedagogical communication 102
peer learning 5
people with disabilities, rights to education of 4
performance-based study 41
personal deficit, sense of 83, 85
person value, Skeggs's concept of 79–80
place-belongingness: concept of 47, 111, 114, 116; feeling of 121; loss of 114
political neoliberal economy 128
post-traumatic stress disorder (PTSD) 125
professional higher education 21
professional validation 87
project learning, problem-oriented 149
properness/non-properness divide 133
proper students, formation of 79
psychiatric diagnostic system 4, 37, 130
psychological distress 2–3
psychosocial difficulties 40, 126, 132, 147
psychosocial problems, related to higher education 1, 2–8, 144; definition of 7; exploration of 6, 9; explosion in the numbers of students with 30; magnitude of 2; mental health issues 2; methodological approach to address 37; research into exploring 36; risk of developing 29; sociological and pedagogical approach to 7; stories about experiencing 36; students' experience of dealing with 41; students' psychosocial problems 4
psychosocial well-being 44
public funding, of education 12
public sector, modernization of 142

qualifications, recognition of 26
qualified workforce, need for 22, 29–30
Quality in the Educational System 22

recognition and belonging, in higher education 2, 4, 14, 41, 52, 97, 151
regulatory discourse 101–102
research-based higher education 21
right for the job 80
right time is on time, notion of 102–105
Rosa, Hartmut 92, 97–98, 105

Sarauw, L. L. 100
school belonging, predictors of 5
'school for all' 21
School of Social Work 89–91
self-belief 126, 129
self-confidence 115, 117
self-correction, project of 89–93
self-efficacy, feeling of 122
self-esteem 85, 117, 122, 135
self-evaluative judgements 46
self-identity, sense of 78
self-modulation, work of 143
self, properties of 81
self-regulation, processes of 11
self-responsibility, discourses of 6
self-transformation, processes of 11
self-valuation, students' stories regarding 86
self-worth, sense of 78
sense of 'suitability', social and cultural construction of 80
shame, in relation to higher education 79; emotion of 140; experiences of 78, 79–81, 85
sick leaves 54, 90, 103–105, 118
Signe, story of 78, 86–89, 93–94, 129, 132, 141
silent revolution 28
site visits 46–47
Smith, Dorothy 8, 139n2; allegory of sociology 39; concept of work knowledge 127
social acceleration 105
social affiliation, of students 11
social belonging 91
social communities, related to higher education 8
social community, study-related 115
social democratic education policy 22
social differentiation 14, 30, 89, 97, 105–107
social inequality 12, 31, 47, 134
social justice 4, 12
social learning, theories of 9

social marginalization, factors related to 37
social mobility 30; and equality 96; and inclusion 20–22
social networks 42–45
social pathologies, representations of 3
social reality, experience of 39
social relations: and networks 152; with teachers 10
social repercussions 112
social reproduction 29, 30
social security 135
social selection, dynamics of 140
social withdrawal, from the study community 113
Social Work programme 93
societal acceleration 100
societal discourses, on student characteristics and responsibilities 94
societal institutions 30, 99
societal recognition 93, 147
solidarity, sense of 121
sorting machine 5, 30, 96, 147
Standards and Guidelines for Quality Assurance in the European Higher Education Area (2015) 33n2
stress-related symptoms 111
students: access to study programmes, regulation of 23; counselling 6, 141; as customers, in an educational market 27; everyday life, activities of 41; experience of "huge confusion" 106; extra work, as reworking accessibility 126–127; 'feeling lost' 83; learning, individualization of 27; as partners 149; perspective, on psychosocial problems related to higher education 37; student life, as a jigsaw of time 97–99; student-centred learning 26–27; transitions, from high school to higher education 5; well-being, in higher education teaching and learning 5
student identities 38, 40, 126; as customers 31; formation of 47; homogenization or conformity of 12, 116; and psychosocial problems 12; role of community in renegotiating 115–118; sense of 11–12
Student Life Project, The 13
student experience, of dealing with psychosocial problems 4; action-oriented 106; with anxiety and

depression 84; everyday life episodes 45; orientation towards a place to visit of their choice 42; orientation towards their everyday life 42; orientation towards their horizontal and vertical life situation 42; orientation towards their study environment 42; orientation towards their use of personal strategies and ways of finding support 42–43; recognition, loneliness and communities 122–123; representations of 6; visit at a chosen location 46–47

students' negotiations of self, poetic representations of 51–53, 144; aesthetic use of language 53; analysis of transcripts and observational notes 52; *Battle with all I've got* (Alicia) 70; *Being talked down to* (Eva) 65; *The big difference* (Christine) 69; *In control* (Sofie) 57; *Forever in my head* (Aron) 73; *The good student* (Jenny) 56; *Huge progress* (Jenny) 66; *I hate dressing up* (Dea) 58; *Me as a student* (Alexander) 55; *A memoir to myself* (Jamie) 60; *Muddled and murky* (Esther) 61; *My cheering squad* (Beate) 62, 64, 67; *My life as a student* (Kenneth) 76; *Not enough nerds* (Beate) 72; *Not really there* (Vera) 54; *One thing a day I can do* (Laura) 59; self-reflection and self-negotiation 52; *Straight-A student* (Jamie) 63; struggle for belonging 52; *Things may turn out well again* (Ida) 75; *Those two girls* (Louise) 68; *Two poles* (Dea) 74; *Wired up differently* (Oscar) 71

Study Life Project 110–111
study programmes: monitoring and control of 28; right for 80
subjectification, power dynamics of 133
suitability, sense of 80
symptoms of inequality 6, 80

teaching discourse 101–102
tertiary education 22
time: for becoming 119–120; as social differentiation 105–107; sociology of 97; structure in higher education 100
timescapes: concept of 98, 120, 123; in higher education 101, 142; influence of 111
Tinto's student integration model 5
transnational organizations 28

U90 (educational planning) programme 22
un-belonging, cases of 12, 116, 118, 122
unemployment rate, discourse about 32
UNESCO 26
United Nations Convention on the Rights of Persons with Disabilities (2006) 4
universal educational timeline 123
university education 21; mental health crisis 3; reforms for development of 29

valuation, students' stories regarding 86
vocational education 118–119
vulnerable (asynchronous) students 107

'weak role', notion of being in 86–89
welfare state: ideals of 21–22; modernization of 23
well-being: elements of 83, 129; feeling of 122
Wenger, E. 111
William, story of 118–121, 123
wonder, politics of 38
work: concept of 128, 143; knowledge, concept of 127, 136

Youth Commission 22